PROXY TARGETS
Civilians in the War in Burundi

Human Rights Watch
New York · Washington · London · Brussels

ISBN 1-56432-179-7
Library of Congress Catalog Card Number: 98-84611

Addresses for Human Rights Watch
350 Fifth Avenue, 34th Floor, New York, NY 10118-3299
Tel: (212) 290-4700, Fax: (212) 736-1300, E-mail: hrwnyc@hrw.org

1522 K Street, N.W., #910, Washington, DC 20005-1202
Tel: (202) 371-6592, Fax: (202) 371-0124, E-mail: hrwdc@hrw.org

33 Islington High Street, N1 9LH London, UK
Tel: (171) 713-1995, Fax: (171) 713-1800, E-mail: hrwatchuk@gn.apc.org

15 Rue Van Campenhout, 1000 Brussels, Belgium
Tel: (2) 732-2009, Fax: (2) 732-0471, E-mail: hrwatcheu@gn.apc.org

Web Site Address: http://www.hrw.org

Listserv address: To subscribe to the list, send an e-mail message to
majordomo@igc.apc.org with "subscribe hrw-news" in the body of the message
(leave the subject line blank).

Human Rights Watch is dedicated to
protecting the human rights of people around the world.

We stand with victims and activists to prevent
discrimination, to uphold political freedom, to protect people from inhumane
conduct in wartime, and to bring offenders to justice.

We investigate and expose
human rights violations and hold abusers accountable.

We challenge governments and those who hold power to end abusive practices
and respect international human rights law.

We enlist the public and the international
community to support the cause of human rights for all.

HUMAN RIGHTS WATCH

ACKNOWLEDGMENTS

This report, based on findings from a mission to Burundi during 1997, was written by Timothy Longman, consultant to Human Rights Watch. Molly Bingham, consultant to Human Rights Watch, assisted with the mission and photographed the images contained in this report. The report was edited by Peter Takirambudde, executive director of the Africa division of Human Rights Watch, Alison Des Forges, consultant to Human Rights Watch, Janet Fleischman, Washington director of the Africa division, Scott Campbell, consultant to Human Rights Watch, Peter Bouckaert, Orville Schell fellow, Wilder Tayler, general counsel, Dinah PoKempner, deputy general counsel, and Michael McClintock, deputy program director. Production assistance was provided by Ariana Pearlroth, associate for the Africa division of Human Rights Watch, Patrick Minges, publications director, and Fitzroy Hepkins, mail manager.

CONTENTS

I. SUMMARY AND RECOMMENDATIONS

The civil war in Burundi is above all else a war against civilians. The conflict ostensibly pits a ruling military and political elite from the minority Tutsi group against insurgents from the majority Hutu group, but in practice, the contenders fight few direct battles and instead carry on combat indirectly through attacks on civilians. Since the civil war began in 1993, the participants in the conflict have consistently targeted Burundi's civilian population for killing, rape, injury, and robbery.

Abuses by the Armed Forces of Burundi

When Major Pierre Buyoya, a former president of Burundi, seized power from a paralyzed civilian government in a July 1996 coup, he claimed that he was seeking to put a stop to the bloodshed that began three years earlier with the murder of Burundi's first popularly elected Hutu president Melchior Ndadaye. Since the coup, however, the armed forces of Burundi have engaged in massive violations of human rights. In a program dubbed "regroupment," the armed forces ordered the rural Hutu population in large areas of the country into camps where they could be more effectively monitored and controlled. To drive people into the regroupment camps, the armed forces indiscriminately attacked civilians, burned their homes, and engaged in extensive rape and beating. The armed forces killed hundreds of civilians who resisted entering the camps. In vast areas of the country where camps have been created, not a single home remains standing.

More than three hundred thousand people have been concentrated in the regroupment camps in crowded and unsanitary conditions. Thousands inside the camps have died from malnutrition and disease, while hundreds of others have been summarily executed. In some cases, soldiers have forced camp residents to work for them and to provide them with the crops from their fields. While the government has responded to international pressure by closing some camps in provinces in northern Burundi where insurgent activity has been brought under control, they have created new camps in regions of renewed insecurity in the south of the country.

Outside the regions of regroupment, government forces have killed and injured civilians in military operations purportedly directed at insurgents. They have also selectively murdered people whom they believed could organize opposition to the government, particularly Hutu with wealth or education, a pattern of violence employed in Burundi during government-sponsored massacres in 1972 that left an estimated 200,000 Hutu dead. Those suffering from chronic malnutrition have also been targeted for violence, because of the belief among the armed forces that malnutrition is evidence of having lived in rebel-controlled areas where food is scarce. In one case, women seeking nutritional supplements for themselves and their children shaved their heads so that they could not be identified by their blond hair, a sign of severe malnutrition. Throughout the country, the armed forces have engaged in rape, arbitrary arrest, looting, and destruction of property. While government forces have eliminated insurgent activity in some parts of the country, they have done so at the cost of the lives of thousands and the human rights of hundreds of thousands of others.

Abuses by Insurgent Groups

Insurgent groups fighting government forces have also violated basic principles of humanitarian law. Like the armed forces, the leading insurgent group, the Forces for the Defense of Democracy (Forces pour la Défense de la Démocratie, FDD), has also attacked and summarily executed civilians. Since they claim to be defending the interests of the majority Hutu population and have little political interest in alienating those they hope will support their cause, the FDD and other insurgent groups have primarily targeted Tutsi, but the insurgent groups have also attacked Hutu civilians, particularly those they accuse of collaboration with the regime, such as government officials. In an April 1997 offensive in southern Burundi, the FDD massacred both Hutu and Tutsi civilians in several communities. The FDD and other insurgent groups have killed far fewer people than have government forces, in part because they are less well armed and in part because the group they attack most—Tutsi civilians—are themselves a relatively small part of the population and generally well defended by the armed forces. To meet their own needs, the insurgents often pillage the crops and other property of civilians. They have compelled some civilians to live in areas under their control as virtual hostages, sometimes obliging these civilians to farm for them or to provide them with other labor. The insurgents have also engaged in extensive destruction of property and in the rape and injury of civilians.

In addition to the FDD, there are several smaller groups of insurgents, including the Party for the Liberation of the Hutu People (Parti pour la Liberation du Peuple Hutu, Palipehutu) and the Front for National Liberation (Front pour la Liberation Nationale, FROLINA).[1] In July and August 1997, the FDD fought the Palipehutu in the northern provinces of Cibitoke and Bubanza in battles that killed some 600 civilians and displaced more than thirty thousand others.

Civilians throughout Burundi told Human Rights Watch that they feel trapped between the sides in the conflict. If they provide support to the FDD or other

---

[1]At the time field research was conducted for this report, FROLINA was observing a truce against government forces, but they ended that truce in late November 1997.

insurgent groups, they could be arrested and killed by the armed forces. If they refuse to support the insurgents, they fear they will be targeted as collaborators.

Militarization of Society

President Buyoya has overseen a massive expansion of the armed forces and a militarization of the general society. The armed forces of Burundi have made extensive acquisitions of arms, despite a regional embargo on Burundi. The armed forces have also nearly doubled in size from 20-25,000 to more than 40,000. This expansion has been accomplished by reducing the period of training from one year to three months and by recruiting women, students, and boys as young as ten years old. Thousands of young men and boys who were members of Tutsi youth gangs in Bujumbura and other cities have been conscripted into the armed forces and, after three months of training, given arms and dispatched with little supervision, sometimes charged with guarding the Hutu population they had previously terrorized. Since virtually all the new recruits have been Tutsi, according to the armed forces' own admission, the dominance of one ethnic group in the armed forces, which were already largely Tutsi, is now even more pronounced.

The armed forces have also provided military training and arms to Tutsi civilians in a "civil self-defense" program launched following a major FDD offensive in southern Burundi in April 1997. They distributed arms to civilians in the southern province of Bururi in May and they began training civilian militia in Bujumbura in June.

The armed forces have also organized adult Hutu men into civilian patrols in order to better control their movements. Throughout much of the country, the Hutu civilians patrol nightly, supposedly to combat the insurgents but also to keep them from providing assistance to opponents of the government.

The International Context

Strife in Burundi has long affected and been affected by conflict in neighboring states as the slaughter of Hutu or Tutsi in one country stokes fears and hatreds in another. Tutsi refugees from Rwanda were important, both as perpetrators and as victims, in violence in Burundi in late 1993, while Hutu refugees from Burundi participated in killing of Tutsi during the Rwandan genocide of 1994. Soldiers of the former Rwandan army (ex-Forces Armées Rwandaises, ex-FAR) and militia responsible for the Rwandan genocide assisted and trained together with the FDD in Zaire. The government of Burundi reportedly supported the Alliance of Democratic Forces for the Liberation of Congo-Zaire (Alliance des Forces Démocratiques pour la Libération du Congo-Zaire, ADFL) in its battles against the Zairian army and its ex-FAR allies. The predominantly Tutsi ADFL attacked, killed, and chased home Hutu refugees from Burundi as well as from Rwanda and hunted down those who fled into the forests of the Congo.[2]

A coalition of regional leaders condemned the coup that brought Buyoya to power and for some sixteen months attempted to use economic sanctions to force peace negotiations and a return to constitutional government. In January 1998, Buyoya was continuing to participate in peace talks, but no lasting agreement had been reached, and regional leaders appeared ready to admit that the sanctions had not worked. Several regional states withdrew from the sanctions in 1997 (some only temporarily), and others were allowing significant violations of the sanctions.

Other governments from outside the immediate region have condemned specific policies of the Buyoya regime, such as regroupment, but have not been clear in denouncing the coup. Distracted by the crisis in Zaire, these governments welcomed Buyoya as an apparent moderate in an increasingly polarized situation, a force for stability in a dangerously precarious region, but this perspective overlooks the widespread human rights violations that have been carried out by the Buyoya regime.

The Mission

Researchers from Human Rights Watch investigated abuses in ten of the sixteen provinces of Burundi in June and July 1997. They interviewed administrative and military officials, opposition politicians, representatives of United Nations agencies and international nongovernmental organizations (NGOs), church representatives, human rights activists, and many ordinary citizens. Although President Buyoya refused Human Rights Watch's repeated requests for an interview, the ministers of justice and interior, the spokesperson for the army, six governors, five assistant governors, nine communal administrators, and many military officers met with the researchers, as did deposed president, Sylvestre Ntibatunganya, leaders of several predominantly Hutu political parties, and a representative in Nairobi of the National Council for the Defense of Democracy (Conseil National de la Défense de la Démocratie, CNDD), the political wing of the FDD.

Human Rights Watch was able to work in most areas where widespread abuses have been reported, including parts of Bururi, Makamba, Bubanza, and

---

[2]Human Rights Watch and Fédération Internationale des Ligues des Droits de l'Homme, Democratic Republic of Congo, "What Kabila is Hiding: Civilian Killings and Impunity in Congo," vol. 9, no. 5(A) (October 1997); Human Rights Watch and Fédération Internationale des Ligues des Droits de l'Homme, Zaire, "Attacked by All Sides: Civilians and the War in Eastern Zaire," vol. 9, no. 1(A) (March 1997).

Bujumbura-Rural provinces where few foreign observers have traveled. Security concerns prevented the researchers from visiting Cibitoke province, the commune of Nyanza-Lac in Makamba, and the parts of Bururi and the Kibira Forest controlled by the FDD. The research team visited regroupment camps in Bubanza, Bururi, Karuzi, Kayanza, Makamba, and Muramvya provinces.

Because of security concerns and a need to protect sources, the citations from interviews in this report generally do not mention names and sometimes do not mention specific locations. With the exception of government administrators and a few others in official positions, researchers guaranteed anonymity to those interviewed. For the same reasons, Human Rights Watch researchers traveled without military escort and did not conduct interviews in the presence of soldiers or government officials.

Recommendations

Government and Armed Forces of Burundi
Human Rights Watch recommends that the government and armed forces of Burundi:

- Immediately end the practices of torture, summary execution, "disappearances," and rape by the armed forces, police, and militia.

- Investigate allegations of summary executions, rape, beatings, torture, excessive force, and other abuses by the armed forces, and punish those responsible for such abuses in accordance with internationally accepted procedures.

- Respect international humanitarian law and human rights law, prohibiting the targeting of civilians and civilian objects in military operations, indiscriminate attacks, looting and unnecessary destruction of civilian property.

- Dismantle the regroupment camps and end all practices of forced relocation of civilian populations.

- Allow freedom of movement and residence, so that displaced people and those subjected to regroupment policies can return to their homes if they so wish.

- Compensate those who have lost homes and possessions during the implementation of the regroupment policy.

- End recruitment and conscription of those under the age of eighteen into the armed forces. Conscription should be enforced only through procedures established in law, and without resort to the use of force.

- Cease political detention, torture, and summary execution.

- Discontinue the use of landmines, and clear landmines now in place.

- Immediate steps must be taken to disarm and dismantle Tutsi paramilitary forces hitherto acting with the acquiescence or in association with the armed forces. Investigate allegations of abuses committed by paramilitary forces, and bring those responsible for abuses to justice.

- Immediately end all forms of forced labor, including the use of regroupment camp residents as labor for the armed forces.

- Cooperate with human rights monitors, and facilitate their access to all parts of the country.

FDD and Other Rebel Groups
Human Rights Watch recommends that the FDD and other armed rebel groups:
- Immediately end the practices of torture, summary execution, "disappearances," and rape.

- Respect international humanitarian law, prohibiting targeting of civilians and civilian objects, rape, torture, indiscriminate attacks on civilians, and destruction or looting of civilian property.

- Refrain from taking food or non-food items, directly or indirectly, from civilians. Any supplies taken by rebel forces should be paid for.

- Cease using civilians for forced labor, and coercing civilians to remain within rebel-controlled areas.

- Discontinue the use of landmines and clear those landmines already emplaced.

- Allow freedom of movement and residence in the areas under rebel control.

- Cooperate with human rights monitors, and facilitate their access to all parts of the country.

The United Nations

- Impose an international arms embargo on the sale or supply of arms and ammunition, as well as military materiel and services, against all sides to the conflict. The embargo should be complemented by enforcement measures including the deployment of military observers at key airstrips and crossing points in Burundi and neighboring countries and the reactivation of the U.N. International Commission of Inquiry on arms trafficking (Rwanda) and extending its mandate to include Burundi.

- Expand the United Nations Human Rights Field Operation in Burundi to permit more human rights monitors and unhindered access to all areas of the country. Its operations outside of Bujumbura should be strengthened to allow consistent monitoring of abuses in all provinces, particularly in areas where large numbers of civilians are being targeted by all sides, including Bujumbura-Rural, Cibitoke, Bubanza, Makamba, and Bururi.

- The U.N. Secretary General should request that U.N. agencies work with Burundians who have been internally displaced by being confined to regroupment camps.

- Consider expanding the mandate of the International Criminal Tribunal for Rwanda to include crimes against humanity committed by all sides in Burundi.

- The U.N. Secretary General's special representative on the impact of armed conflict on children, Clara Otunnu, should promptly investigate the use of children under eighteen as soldiers, as well as the impact in general of armed conflict on the children of Burundi.

- The U.N. Committee on the Rights of the Child should conduct an on-site investigation into the situation of children used as soldiers.

- UNICEF should monitor conditions for children in the regroupment camps and the situation of children used as soldiers, and work with the government, NGOs and relief agencies to improve conditions.

- The U.N. Working Group on a Draft Optional Protocol to the Convention on the Rights of the Child on Involvement of Children in Armed Conflicts should seek to raise to eighteen the minimum age at which people may be recruited into armed forces and participate in hostilities (whether that recruitment is voluntary or compulsory, and whether it is into governmental or nongovernmental armed forces). African states should be encouraged to participate actively in the working group.

The International Community

- Ensure that all the forced regroupment camps are immediately closed, and that the government and military authorities impose no restrictions on civilians from returning to their homes.

- Vigorously and publicly condemn human rights abuses by all sides to the conflict, and call on all sides to cease committing gross violations of international human rights and humanitarian law.

- Support an international arms embargo against all sides to the conflict in Burundi.

- Urge neighboring countries to refrain from forcibly repatriating genuine refugees to Burundi, and call on the Armed Forces of Burundi to halt any efforts to forcibly repatriate Burundian refugees from neighboring countries.

- Continue to prevent all bilateral and multilateral assistance to the government of Burundi, except humanitarian assistance, until the following minimum benchmarks are met: military attacks on civilians cease and those responsible are investigated and prosecuted; the regroupment camps and all forms of forced resettlement are entirely ended; and ensure that Burundian army involvement in forcible repatriation of refugees is halted. In addition, concrete progress should be made toward establishing an inclusive political system in which the rights of free expression and association of all communities are respected, and harassment of opposition politicians, journalists and human rights activists is ended.

- Once aid to the government of Burundi resumes, make a priority on supporting efforts to build an independent and impartial judicial system, with broad recruitment of judges, lawyers and magistrates in terms of regional, ethnic and gender diversity.

- In all discussions with insurgent forces, insist upon the enforcement of human rights and humanitarian law, particularly involving the protection of civilian populations and other human rights guarantees.

II. BACKGROUND TO THE CIVIL WAR

Background

The current civil war in Burundi represents the most prolonged period of violent conflict in a country whose recent history has been marked by periodic explosions of deadly inter-ethnic strife. The current conflict, like others before in Burundi and in adjacent Rwanda, takes the shape of a struggle between two ethnic groups: the Hutu, who form approximately 85 percent of the population, and the Tutsi, who make up around 15 percent. The ethnic coloration of the conflict, however, only disguises and embitters what is fundamentally a battle over political and economic power much like similar struggles elsewhere in the world.

Scholars debate the exact meaning of the labels "Hutu," "Tutsi," and "Twa," in pre-colonial Burundi, but they agree that all three groups shared a single language, religious practices, and political system and lived intermingled within a territory that they all knew as Burundi.[3] The terms may have derived in part from occupational differences, since most Tutsi raised cattle, the sign of wealth in Burundian society, most Hutu raised crops, and most Twa lived from hunting and gathering. The Twa, today less than 1 percent of the population, are not numerous enough to play a significant role in present-day conflicts at the national level, though they have figured importantly either as killers or as victims in some regions. A fourth group, the Ganwa, an elite comprised of descendants of past rulers, were considered neither Hutu nor Tutsi and also very small in numbers. Although both Twa and Ganwa were historically set apart from the other groups, the distinctions between Hutu and Tutsi were more flexible. Individuals could move from one category to the other, depending on their wealth and political prestige, and political conflicts generally cut across lines of identity rather than reinforcing them.[4]

Colonial rulers, first Germans and, after World War I, Belgians, sought to rule through the existing monarchy, but their policies served to eliminate the complexity

---

[3]Jean-Pierre Chrétien has argued that Hutu and Tutsi as categories were fundamentally colonial constructions, (c.f., "Manipulations de l'histoire, manipulations des identités et violence politique: Les enseignements du cas burundais," in Bogumil Jewsiewicki and J. Létoruneau, eds. *Constructions identitaires: questionnements théoriques et études de cas* (Québec, 1992), pp. 11-29). Other scholars such as René Lemarchand, Catharine Newbury, and Alison Des Forges contend that Hutu and Tutsi existed as terms describing individuals in Rwanda and Burundi prior to colonial rule, but that the use of these labels to describe categories followed changes introduced by colonialism.

[4]René Lemarchand, *Burundi: Ethnocide as Discourse and Practice* (Cambridge: Cambridge University Press, 1994), pp. 6-16.

and flexibility of the pre-colonial social and political systems and to change Hutu, Tutsi, and Twa into rigid ethnic categories. Applying their own racist ideas about a hierarchy among peoples, colonial administrators concluded that Tutsi, Hutu and Twa were distinct racial groups. They considered the Tutsi, who stereotypically were tall and thin, with lighter skin and narrow features, more closely related to Europeans and therefore superior to Hutu and Twa who looked less like the colonialists. They viewed the Ganwa, few in number, as a somewhat more privileged group of Tutsi. Putting their ideas into operation in a system known as indirect rule, the colonialists favored the Tutsi and helped them to gain more control over the Hutu. They excluded Hutu not just from administrative posts but also from higher education, thus creating conditions for Tutsi domination far into the future.[5]

In neighboring Rwanda, where the demographics and colonial policies were similar, the Belgian administration changed its practice in the mid-1950s and began permitting Hutu to assume a larger role in public life and assuring them more places in educational institutions. Dissatisfied with the slow pace of reforms, Hutu rose up against Tutsi rule beginning in 1959, ousted the monarch and killed or drove into exile thousands of Tutsi. Between 1959 and 1962, nearly all administrative positions were transferred from Tutsi to Hutu, and Rwanda gained independence in 1962 with a government controlled by Hutu.[6]

In the years immediately after Burundi regained its independence from Belgium in 1962, its ruler, Mwambutsa, sought to avoid a similar revolution by balancing Tutsi and Hutu interests. But as conflicts between the groups increased, he became increasingly linked with Tutsi interests and lost his role of neutral arbiter. A Rwandan Tutsi refugee assassinated the first Hutu prime minister three days after his appointment in January 1965. Mwambutsa hoped to appease the Hutu population and maintain control by permitting legislative elections, but after predominately Hutu parties won a decisive majority, he refused to name another Hutu prime minister. A few months later, in October 1965, Hutu soldiers and gendarmes killed the Tutsi prime minister in an attempted coup and forced Mwambutsa to flee the country. The army subsequently executed several Hutu military officers and nearly all prominent Hutu politicians and began to purge Hutu from the ranks of the armed forces. Hutu in Muramvya province attacked Tutsi

---

[5]Lemarchand, *Burundi: Ethnocide as Discourse and Practice*, pp. 58-76; Alison Des Forges, "Burundi: Failed Coup or Creeping Coup," *Current History*, May 1994.

[6]For a comparison of late colonial and early post-independence histories of Rwanda and Burundi, see René Lemarchand, *Rwanda and Burundi* (London: Pall Mall, 1970).

residents, and Tutsi soldiers and civilian militia responded by massacring some 5,000 Hutu. Mwambutsa attempted to rule from Congo, but eventually abdicated in favor of his son. The new king failed to establish his authority, and within months of his installation in July 1966, Tutsi military officers deposed him and installed Captain Michel Michombero as president.[7]

In April 1972, Hutu insurgents attacked and captured the southern towns of Rumonge and Nyanza-Lac along the shore of Lake Tanganyika and killed many Tutsi residents. The army easily quelled the uprising but used it as a pretext for massive slaughter of Hutu. In what Lemarchand has dubbed a "selective genocide," the army and Tutsi militia killed an estimated 100,000 people, targeting in particular teachers, students, clergy, and other Hutu intellectuals as well as Hutu soldiers. According to Lemarchand and Martin, "The aim was to decapitate not only the rebellion but Hutu society as well, and in the process lay the foundation of an entirely new social order. ... The annihilation of the Hutu elites ... effectively eliminated all potential threats to Tutsi hegemony from the Hutu, at least for the next generation."[8] In addition to the thousands killed, the attacks by the armed forces and militia drove several hundred thousand Hutu into exile in neighboring countries, where some later organized guerrilla movements. Memories of the 1972 massacres have powerfully shaped subsequent Hutu political thought and action, both inside and outside Burundi. Many Hutu believe they will remain vulnerable to similar attacks as long as Tutsi maintain a monopoly on political and military power.[9]

---

[7]Lemarchand, *Burundi: Ethnocide as Discourse and Practice*, pp. 58-75.

[8]René Lemarchand and David Martin, *Selective Genocide in Burundi*, (London: Minority Rights Group, 1973); René Lemarchand, "The Hutu-Tutsi Conflict in Burundi," in Jack Nusan Porter, ed., *Genocide and Human Rights: A Global Anthology*, (University Press of America, 1982), pp. 195-217; and Christian Thibon, "Les origines historiques de la violence politique au Burundi," in André Guichaoua, *Les crises politiques au Burundi et au Rwanda (1993-1994)* (Lille: Université des Sciences et Technologies, 1995), pp. 57-58. Citation from Lemarchand and Martin, pp. 18-19.

[9]Reginald Kay, *Burundi since the genocide*, (London: Minority Rights Group, 1987); Thibon, "Les origines historiques de la violence politique au Burundi," pp. 57-61; and Lemarchand, *Burundi: Ethnocide as Discourse and Practice*, pp. 76-105. Lisa H. Malkki, *Purity and Exile: Violence, Memory, and National Cosmology Among Hutu Refugees in Tanzania* (Chicago: University of Chicago Press, 1995), offers an excellent analysis of the persistence of anger and fear among Burundian Hutu refugees over the 1972 massacres and how this anger and fear continues to shape their political thought and identities.

In the two decades following the 1972 massacres, Hutu were almost entirely excluded from political office, the military, schools, and other opportunities. Lt. Col. Jean-Baptiste Bagaza replaced Micombero as president in a 1976 coup, but continued the policy of discrimination against Hutu. He stressed national unity and banned all references to ethnicity as incitements to racial hatred, effectively preventing Hutu from complaining about the discrimination they faced. President Bagaza also launched a campaign against Catholic and Protestant churches, expelling 80 percent of foreign missionaries and limiting church activities, because he suspected the churches of radicalizing the Hutu.[10]

Major Pierre Buyoya replaced Bagaza in a coup in 1987 . When Hutu rose up the next year in Ngozi and Kirundo provinces along the Rwanda border and killed several thousand Tutsi, Buyoya permitted the army to restore "peace and order" by using helicopters and armored vehicles to massacre some 20,000 Hutu.[11]

Steps Toward Reconciliation

Buyoya rejected calls for an independent investigation into the 1988 massacres, but he nonetheless shifted the policy direction of the government and sought ways of encouraging reconciliation between Hutu and Tutsi, rather than simply relying on repression to control the Hutu population. He appointed a multi-ethnic commission to study the Hutu-Tutsi question and appointed Hutu to positions in his government. He also restored normal relations with the churches.[12]

Past violence within Burundi, as well as in Rwanda, complicated efforts at reconciliation between Burundi's two main ethnic communities. Members of each group feared violence — even potential annihilation — by the other and felt anger for past sufferings. Tutsi viewed the slaughter of Tutsi in Rwanda following the Tutsi loss of power as a warning and feared that sharing power with Hutu in Burundi would also lead to large-scale killing of Tutsi. Tutsi soldiers associated

---

[10]Lemarchand, *Burundi: Ethnocide as Discourse and Practice*, pp. 106-117; Jean-Pierre Chrétien, "Eglise et Etat au Burundi: les enjeux politiques," *Afrique Contemporaine*, April-May-June 1987, pp. 63-68.

[11]Lemarchand, *Burundi: Ethnocide as Discourse and Practice*, pp. 118-130.

[12]André Guichaoua, "De la transition démocratique à la tourmente ethnique: les ruptures douloureuses de l'ordre paysan au Burundi," in Guichaoua, ed., *Les crises politiques au Burundi et au Rwanda (1993-1994)*, pp. 99-105; and Lemarchand, *Burundi: Ethnocide as Discourse and Practice*, pp. 131-139.

with former president Bagaza and opposed to Buyoya's reforms attempted unsuccessfully to organize coups in November 1989 and again in March 1992.[13]

Hutu keenly remembered the "selective genocide" of Hutu intellectuals in 1972 and feared and distrusted both civilian and military authorities. Hutu who had been driven into exile in Tanzania organized the Party for the Liberation of the Hutu People (Parti pour la Liberation du Peuple Hutu, Palipehutu), which launched several attacks in the northwestern provinces of Bubanza and Cibitoke in 1991 and 1992, killing a number of Tutsi. In each case, the army retaliated against the Hutu population, but they behaved with greater restraint than in 1988.[14]

Despite resistance from many Tutsi, including some soldiers, Buyoya presented a new constitution which won overwhelming approval in a public referendum in 1992. He appointed a Hutu prime minister and scheduled presidential and parliamentary elections in June 1993. Buyoya, who ran as the presidential candidate for the Party of Union for National Progress (Parti de l'Union et du Progrès National, Uprona), a largely Tutsi political party that was formerly the only legal party, won 33 percent of the vote in the June 1 elections, while Melchior Ndadaye, who ran as the candidate for the Front of Burundi Democrats (Front des Démocrates du Burundi, Frodebu), a largely Hutu party, won 65 percent. Although according to diplomatic sources Buyoya had confidently expected to win the election, he accepted defeat and allowed June 29 parliamentary elections to proceed. In these elections, Frodebu won 65 of 81 seats.[15]

On July 2, a group of soldiers attempted to take power. Although Buyoya quickly put down the uprising, the coup attempt showed the extent of dissatisfaction among soldiers and indicated that the armed forces, which Buyoya had not attempted to reform and which remained almost exclusively Tutsi, might well pose problems for his successor.[16]

---

[13]Lemarchand, *Burundi: Ethnocide as Discourse and Practice*, pp. 139-142.

[14]Thibon, "Les origines historiques de la violence politique au Burundi," pp. 58-60.

[15]Lemarchand, *Burundi: Ethnocide as Discourse and Practice*, pp. 178-187; and Human Rights Watch interviews, June and July 1997.

[16]Olivier Delorme and Michel Gaud, "Chronologie Politique du Burundi," *Afrique Contemporaine*, no. 179, July-September 1996, pp. 63-79.

Civilian Government and a Return to Violence

On July 10, 1993, Ndadaye became the first Hutu President of Burundi. In an attempt to win broad-based support, he named a multiparty cabinet with seven Tutsi and fifteen Hutu led by a Tutsi woman prime minister from Uprona, Sylvie Kinigi.[17] As president, Ndadaye made important changes in local administration, installing members of his Frodebu party, and he was planning to separate the gendarmerie (national police) from the army and to increase ethnic and regional diversity in the armed forces. To avert these and other changes, a small group of Tutsi soldiers attempted to seize power on October 21, 1993. They captured and later executed Ndadaye, along with a number of other high ranking civilian political officials, including the president of the national assembly, the president's constitutionally designated successor. Other government officials, including Prime Minister Kinigi, took refuge in various embassies and diplomatic residences. While some military officers supported the putsch, others did not. In addition, the international community strongly condemned the coup and threatened to cut aid unless constitutional government were restored. In the face of firm and consistent opposition from abroad and of the threat of widespread uprisings within the country, the army chief of staff, Col. Jean Bikomagu, declared the coup ended and sent the soldiers back to the barracks.[18]

As news of the murder of Ndadaye spread through Burundi, Hutu government officials and other local leaders directed attacks on Tutsi civilians in which thousands were killed. Anticipating military assault, Hutu blockaded roads in the northern, central, and eastern parts of the country. The army responded with attacks on Hutu, making no distinction between communities involved in violence against Tutsi and those that were not. In a period of only a few weeks, anywhere from 30,000 to 50,000 people were slain, roughly an equal number from each ethnic group. Thousands of Hutu fled into exile, while both Hutu and Tutsi hid in the swamps and forests of the country.[19]

---

[17]Guichaoua, ed., *Les crises politiques au Burundi et au Rwanda (1993-1994)*, pp. 736-737.

[18]Commission Internationale d'Enquête sur les Violations des Droits de l'Homme depuis le 21 Octobre 1993, *Rapport Final* (Paris: FIDH, July 1995); Gaëtan Sebudandi and Pierre-Olivier Richard, *Le drame burundais: Hantise du pouvoir ou tentation suicidaire* (Paris: Karthala, 1996).

[19]Human Rights Watch, *Human Rights Watch World Report 1995* (New York: Human Rights Watch, 1994), p. 13.

An international investigative team sponsored by a coalition of nongovernmental organizations, including Human Rights Watch, found evidence during a visit in Burundi in January and February 1994 that a number of high-ranking military officers had taken part in the murders of Ndadaye and other political officials and in the bloody "pacification campaigns" that left thousands of Hutu dead in the countryside. The International Commission of Inquiry also found evidence that Hutu officials led, facilitated, or permitted massacres of Tutsi civilians.[20] The government of Burundi has tried, condemned to death, and executed six civilians in connection with the 1993 killings, and thousands of others await trail.[21] A group of military officers also stands accused of involvement in the coup attempt, but their trial has experienced repeated delays, and to date no soldiers have been found guilty for involvement in the coup or the subsequent violent repression. Lt. Jean-Paul Kamana, whom the International Commission of Inquiry identified as having commanded the attack on the presidential palace and ordered the murder of Ndadaye, issued a statement in late 1997 from exile in Uganda claiming he had been following the orders of his superiors, including President Buyoya, in carrying out the attack and murder, a charge Buyoya vehemently denied.[22]

Following the coup attempt, the surviving ministers of the Ndadaye government struggled to reconstitute a new government. After several months of negotiation, Cyprien Ntaryamira, the agriculture minister and a Hutu from Frodebu, was appointed president, but he was killed several months later in the same plane crash in Kigali that killed Rwandan President Juvénal Habyarimana, on April 6, 1994. His successor was Sylvestre Ntibantunganya, another Hutu from Frodebu. In September 1994, Frodebu negotiated the Convention of Government, a compromise with the major Tutsi party, Uprona, and the armed forces, providing a five-year mandate to reestablish security and prepare for elections. The Convention of Government established a powerful National Security Council that weakened the authority of the president and parliament and gave Uprona and

---

[20]Commission Internationale d'Enquete, *Rapport Final*, pp. 14-48.

[21]U.N. Department of Humanitarian Affairs, Integrated Regional Information Network (IRIN), "Emergency Update on the Great Lakes," August 14, 1997.

[22]Alfred Wasike, "Ndadaye Murder Plot Exposed," *New Vision*, November 17, 1997; Declaration, Office of the President, "Les Declarations du Lieutenant Kamana Contre le Major Buyoya Pourraient Servir de Pretexte à la Tanzanie pour Attaquer le Burundi," November 20, 1997.

several small Tutsi supremacist parties (parties that argue for a return to exclusive Tutsi control of government) de facto veto power over government decisions. As a result, the government found itself virtually paralyzed, while the armed forces acted with almost complete autonomy.[23]

Following Ndadaye's assassination, some Frodebu officials who fled into exile organized a new armed movement which committed itself to subduing the armed forces in order to make stable democratic government possible.[24] The National Council for the Defense of Democracy (Conseil National pour la Défense de la Démocratie, CNDD) and its armed wing, the Forces for the Defense of Democracy (Forces pour la Défense de la Démocratie, FDD), are led by the former minister of public functions, work, and repatriation of refugees, Léonard Nyangoma. The FDD set up bases among Hutu refugees in Zaire and began a campaign of guerrilla attacks on military and Tutsi civilian targets in Burundi. Over the next several years, the FDD established camps in some of the more remote areas of the country—Kibira National Forest and Ruvubu National Park in the north and the high mountains along the Congo-Nile continental divide in the south. Much of the Hutu population, feeling increasingly frustrated with the impotence of the civilian government, lent support to the FDD in its struggle against the armed forces. Informants in several rural communities told Human Rights Watch that by 1995 or 1996 the CNDD had established a parallel administration in their area and that FDD combatants received material support from residents.[25] Other smaller Hutu rebel groups, including Palipehutu and the National Liberation Front (Front pour

---

[23]Delorme and Gaud, "Chronologie Politique du Burundi."

[24]For a statement of the CNDD's perspective on events in Burundi, see Léonce Ndarubagiye, *Burundi: The Origins of the Hutu-Tutsi Conflict* (Nairobi, 1995). Ndarubagiye writes: "The first objective of the CNDD is the defence of the gains acquired from the June 1993 elections in restoring the people's inalienable rights, notably the right to be ruled by leaders of their choice with a program in accordance with their interests" (p. 81). While Ndarubagiye, himself a Tutsi businessman, claims that the CNDD is multi-ethnic, most observers consider the FDD a Hutu movement, an assessment reinforced by FDD attacks on Tutsi civilians.

[25]Human Rights Watch interviews, June and July 1997.

la Libération Nationale, Frolina), which ended an 18-month unilateral cease-fire in late October 1997, have also engaged in guerrilla attacks.[26]

Beginning in 1994—particularly following the genocide of Tutsi and the killings of moderate Hutu in Rwanda—Tutsi militia and youth gangs began to play a large role in the conflict in Burundi. The slaughter of Tutsi in the weeks following Ndadaye's assassination and continuing attacks by the FDD and its supporters drove Tutsi in many areas of the country to seek protection in camps built around military posts. These camps for internally displaced Tutsi became centers of paramilitary activity, as Tutsi militia, with the backing of soldiers, sought to take revenge on Hutu populations for the death of their family members and loss of property.[27] In Bujumbura and some other cities, Hutu youth also formed gangs and fought Tutsi gangs. Both groups terrorized the population, frequently for criminal as well as political ends. In early 1995, the Tutsi gangs such as the Sans Echec (Without Failure) and Sans Défaite (Without Defeat), with assistance from the armed forces (including arms and training, according to some sources),drove most Hutu out of urban areas into exile in neighboring countries or to refuge within the interior of the country.[28] Today, Bujumbura remains an overwhelmingly Tutsi city, with most of the few remaining Hutu concentrated in refugee camps around the periphery of the city or with families in the hills above the town.

This report makes a distinction between regroupment camps, which are mainly populated by Hutu civilians who were forced into the camps by the military, and internally displaced persons (IDP) camps, which are generally populated by Tutsi civilians displaced by the armed conflict. There were qualitative differences in the creation of, and conditions within, the regroupment camps and the IDP camps, although considerable suffering was a factor for the civilians in both. The camps for the internally displaced (IDP) are distinguished from the regroupment camps, however, by their voluntary nature. While the majority of those in these camps would prefer to live at home if security conditions allowed, they choose to remain

---

[26]"Spokesman says Military Struggle to Resume in Burundi," Front for National Liberation in Burundi, November 22, 1997; "Burundian rebel group claims killing hundreds of government troops," Agence France Presse, November 2, 1997.

[27]Human Rights Watch investigated continuing cases of Tutsi militia activity around refugee camps in Gitega, Ruyigi, and Karuzi. See chapter four.

[28]Human Rights Watch interview, Bujumbura, June 16, 1997. C.f., "Burundi's President Says Genocide Started," Reuters, March 27, 1995; "Tutsi Troops Patrol Bujumbura," Associated Press, March 27, 1995; "Ethnic Violence Wracks Burundi," March 29, 1995.

in the camps because of the safety the camps afford. In contrast to the regroupment camps, people in the IDP camps are free to come and go at will and have the protection of the armed forces.

The Tutsi political parties and the military both used the growing civil unrest to bolster their positions. The Tutsi supremacist parties used increasing militia and gang violence to bring life in Bujumbura to a halt, forcing the replacement of the president of the National Assembly and the prime minister in late 1994 and early 1995, and they maneuvered an increasing number of hard-line Tutsi into political positions, including Antoine Nduwayo, who became prime minister.[29]

As the FDD increased attacks, the armed forces retaliated not just against the guerillas but also against Hutu civilians, killing hundreds of noncombatants in "pacification campaigns" in Bubanza, Gitega, and Cibitoke, where the military suspected that support for the FDD was strong. In March 1995, the army launched a disarmament campaign, which consisted primarily of gathering arms from Hutu gangs. According to some sources, arms gathered from Hutu gangs were subsequently redistributed to Tutsi gangs. Under the guise of the disarmament campaign, the military became actively involved in driving the population out of predominately Hutu neighborhoods in Bujumbura, such as Kamenge, Kinama, and Cibitoke.[30]

Buyoya's Return to Power

By early 1996, the civilian government under President Ntibantunganya had lost effective control of the country. A growing number of political assassinations strengthened the hand of the military.[31] Civilian governors were assassinated in the

---

[29]Deogratias Muvira, "Burundi President Says Crisis Over as Xmas Gift," Reuters, December 28, 1994; Alex Belida, "Burundi Politics," Voice of America, February 8, 1995; "Unrest Flares in Burundi," Associated Press, February 8, 1995; "General Strike Closes Down Burundian Capital," Reuters, February 15, 1995; Deogratias Muvira, "Shots, Blasts in Burundi Capital After Resignation," Reuters, February 15, 1995.

[30]Amnesty International, "Burundi: Struggle for Survival - Immediate Action Vital to Stop Killings, (London: Amnesty International, June 1995); Human Rights Watch interviews, June and July 1997.

[31]In a document prepared in May 1996, Frodebu counted the assassinations of two presidents (including President Ntaryamira, who was killed along with President Habyarimana in a Kigali plane crash by as yet undetermined assailants), four ministers, fifteen parliamentarians, thirteen governors or assistant governors, eighteen communal administrators, and a large number of other political figures since 1993. Parti Sahwanya

northern provinces of Cibitoke, Gitega, Karuzi, Kayana, and Ngozi, all areas where the armed forces believed the FDD to be active, and replaced by military officers who implemented programs to subdue the Hutu population. In early 1996, the military governor of Karuzi initiated the first regroupment program, using extensive violence to drive more than one hundred thousand Hutu from his province into camps in early 1996. Uprona and other Tutsi parties worked closely with the armed forces to undermine President Ntibantunganya and other Frodebu officials. With most Frodebu leaders either dead or in exile, the remaining leaders found themselves almost completely powerless to combat the growing violence and lawlessness in the country.[32]

Following a week of great uncertainty in the capital, the military formally seized power on July 25, 1996, after President Ntibantunganya and other Frodebu leaders took refuge in the German and United States diplomatic residences. The former president, Major Buyoya, was named president again, claiming that he had taken power "only to prevent more ethnic killings." Buyoya presented himself as a comparative moderate who had stepped in to prevent more extreme Tutsi elements, like supporters of ex-president Bagaza, from taking power. He also claimed that he would quickly return the country to democracy. "We have to bring back democracy ... but how long it will take we don't know; it could be 12 months, 18 months or more."[33]

Hutu politicians have challenged Buyoya's claims of moderation, arguing that much of the violence and disorder prior to the coup was orchestrated by the military and its supporters in order to justify a coup. As one Hutu politician told Human Rights Watch, "All these assassinations were to bring Buyoya back."[34] If Tutsi militia and youth gangs have been less active since the coup, it may be because they have accomplished their goal of undermining the civilian government and bringing Tutsi back to power. It may also be that with Buyoya in control, the armed forces have enforced order more rigorously than before. One Frodebu

---

Frodebu, "Genocide en Cours au Burundi: Cas des Intellectuels Hutu," Bujumbura, May 15, 1996.

[32]Human Rights Watch, *Human Rights Watch World Report 1997* (New York: Human Rights Watch, 1996), pp. 20-21; Human Rights Watch interviews, June and July 1997.

[33]Quoted in Donald G. McNeil, "Leader of Coup in Burundi Hints at Tribal Reconciliation," *New York Times*, July 27, 1997.

[34]Human Rights Watch interview, Bujumbura, June 16, 1997.

leader observed, "The army is charged with protecting the institutions and the population. How is it they were incapable of doing so under Ntibantunganya but are capable under Buyoya?"[35]

Although Buyoya and the military took power without bloodshed, they have used their power subsequently to kill, rape, injure, and drive from their homes hundreds of thousands of civilians. Although the coup brought greater calm to the overwhelmingly Tutsi capital, it resulted in greater violence to the countryside as the regroupment program was expanded and the armed forces used extensive violence to subdue the population. While in recent months open violence has decreased in some rural areas, the relative calm results largely from exhaustion and repression rather than from a successful resolution to the causes of unrest.

As part of a military escort, soldiers remain prepared to shoot at all times at any sign of a threat.

Although much of the international community could not decide how to react to the coup, African leaders strongly condemned it. Regional heads of state decided at a meeting held in Arusha, Tanzania, on August 9, 1996, to impose sanctions, closing their borders to all trade with Burundi.[36] While immediately after taking power, President Buyoya suspended the National Assembly and banned

---

[35]Human Rights Watch interview, Bujumbura, June 25, 1997.

[36]Barbara Crossette, "Rwanda Joins Effort to Isolate Burundi," *New York Times*, August 9, 1996.

political party activity, a few months later he allowed parties and the assembly to resume some of their functions, apparently in response to the sanctions.[37] Under pressure from humanitarian agencies, the sanctions were relaxed somewhat in April 1997 to allow delivery of food and medicines.[38]

In the months following the coup, the government extended the violent regroupment program, displacing population and creating camps in parts of Bubanza, Cibitoke, Kayanza, Muramvya, Bujumbura-Rural, and Bururi provinces as detailed in chapter three. In many rural areas where the regroupment policy was not carried out, the armed forces used extensive repression and violence to subdue the population.

Events in neighboring Zaire served to bolster Buyoya's position. In late 1996, an ethnic campaign against the Zairian Tutsi in South Kivu known as the Banyamulenge backfired when the Banyamulenge took up arms and began to attack those who had attacked them, government troops and civilian militia, including some Rwandan and Burundian Hutu refugees. The Banyamulenge joined with other groups opposed to the rule of President Mobutu Sese Seko to form the Alliance of Democratic Forces for the Liberation of Congo-Zaire (ADFL) and, with assistance from Rwanda and Uganda, quickly seized control of much of eastern Zaire, including all areas bordering on Burundi. Among the initial targets of the ADFL were the refugee camps for Hutu who had fled violence in Rwanda and Burundi. The camps housed many legitimate refugees but also served as a base for former members of the Rwandan army (ex-FAR) and the Interahamwe militia who had taken part in the Rwandan genocide in 1994. These Hutu extremists launched attacks in both Rwanda and Zaire, and they increasingly supported the FDD in its operations in Burundi.[39] Although the CNDD spokesperson in Nairobi denied that the FDD had used military bases in Zaire,[40] most observers agree that the insurgents had used the camps there as launching points for attacks on Burundi.

---

[37]Ibid.

[38]"Sanctions Against Burundi Eased," Reuters, April 17, 1997.

[39]See Human Rights Watch and Fédération Internationale des Ligues des Droits de l'Homme, Zaire, "Attacked by All Sides: Civilians and the War in Eastern Zaire," vol. 9, no. 1(A), March 1997; Human Rights Watch, "Zaire: Transition, War, and Human Rights," vol. 9, no. 2(A), April 1997.

[40]Human Rights Watch interview in Nairobi, June 4, 1997.

The ADFL victory in Zaire, which was renamed the Democratic Republic of Congo, severely weakened the position of the FDD. By forcing refugees to return to Burundi, the ADFL eliminated important bases for the FDD and other insurgent groups in Zaire. Many of those repatriated were not allowed to return to their homes but were forced into the heavily guarded regroupment camps, where their ability to lend support to the insurgents was limited. Driven from Zaire, the FDD was forced to establish new bases in Tanzania. According to diplomats in Burundi, the FDD offensive in the southern provinces of Bururi and Makamba, which began in March 1997, marked the shift in FDD operations to Tanzania and an attempt by the FDD to demonstrate that it remained a powerful force in Burundi.[41]

In the year since his return to power, Buyoya has taken firm control over the armed forces and the administration. He has replaced many Hutu with Tutsi, thus intensifying a process begun after Ndadaye's assassination and reinforcing the predominantly Tutsi character of the power structure. The cabinet does include a number of Hutu, but the most powerful ministries are reserved for Tutsi, particularly military officers, and lower levels of government are now overwhelmingly Tutsi. Of 121 communal administrators in April 1997, only thirty-one were Hutu, twenty-two of whom belonged to Uprona, Buyoya's political party. In parastatal corporations and such ministries as education, where Hutu figured importantly several years ago, Tutsi have now taken the positions of power.[42]

Buyoya has faced some opposition from factions within the military and Tutsi political parties. Former president Bagaza and his political party, the Party for National Recovery (Parti pour le Redressement National, Parena), have led criticism of Buyoya. Buyoya countered his opposition by placing Bagaza under house arrest in January 1997 and by arresting other Tutsi political leaders, including some from his own party at various times over the past year. Opposition came to a head in May 1997 when it became public knowledge that the Buyoya regime had been engaging in talks with the FDD in Rome, but Buyoya quickly halted protests by Tutsi students and others, thus demonstrating his continuing

---

[41]Human Rights Watch interviews, Bujumbura, June 7 and 10, 1997.

[42]Anonymous document, "La politique intérieure de Buyoya: Nouveau visage de l'administration du territoire après le coup d'état du Major Buyoya (le 25 juillet 1996)," Bujumbura, April 2, 1997; anonymous document, "Nouveau visage du Ministere de l'Enseignement Secondaire, Superieur et Recherche Scientifique," Bujumbura, May 10, 1997.

strength within both the military and the government. In November 1997, Bagaza was charged with organizing a plot to kill Buyoya.[43]

Formal negotiations with the CNDD were scheduled in Arusha in August 1997, but the government pulled out shortly before the talks were to begin, citing security concerns. The parties in the conflict engaged in less formal discussions the next month in a meeting sponsored by UNESCO in Paris, and at the beginning of 1998, the parties were set to resume negotiations under heavy pressure from regional and other international actors.[44]

---

[43]"Burundian former president accused of assassination plot," Agence France Presse, November 21, 1997.

[44]U.N. Department of Humanitarian Affairs, IRIN, "Emergency Update No. 258 on the Great Lakes," September 27-29, 1997.

III. "WE ARE LIKE PRISONERS HERE":
FORCED DISPLACEMENT OF CIVILIAN POPULATIONS

The military officers who organized the July 1996 coup in Burundi claimed that their seizure of power was necessary to bring order to an increasingly chaotic country. However, since the coup, the armed forces of Burundi have engaged in widespread violations of human rights, humanitarian law, and the law of war, particularly in rural areas. From September 1996 through March 1997, the armed forces killed, raped, and tortured thousands of Hutu civilians and pillaged and destroyed countless homes during the implementation of a program known as "regroupment" which has forcibly displaced hundreds of thousands of civilians. Today, the government of Burundi continues to force more than 200,000 Hutu civilians to remain in life-threatening conditions in regroupment camps in clear violation of the laws of war and the rights to freedom of movement and freedom from arbitrary detention. The armed forces continue to engage in rape, torture, extrajudicial execution, and pillage in and around the regroupment camps.

As one NGO worker summarizes the current state of the regroupment program:

> Hutus are officially protected from rebels by the army in those camps; in reality they are prisoners. They are very like concentration camps. [People] cannot leave them, because, if so, they are shot; they have no land to work in, no clean clothing, they have nothing. Scabies and hunger are present in every regroupment camp. Furthermore, there is a dysentery epidemic all over the country.[45]

Forced Regroupment Programs and International Law

The government of Burundi's "regroupment" program has forced thousands of Hutu civilians out of their homes and into guarded camps. Similar programs had been implemented by the French in Indochina (from 1946 to 1954), and in Algeria in the 1950s; by the British in Malaya and Kenya in the same period; by the United States and its South Vietnamese allies in the 1960s; and in Guatemala in the 1980s. The regroupment system allows the military to monitor the civilian population closely and to restrict their freedoms of movement, association, and speech, in an attempt to prevent the suspect population from providing support for armed rebel movements. In Burundi, the Hutu are the suspect population, and their concentration in camps is intended to cut them off from rebel groups such as the Forces for the Defense of Democracy (Forces pour la Défense de la Démocratie,

---

[45]Personal communication from Bujumbura, December 16, 1997.

FDD), which had apparently gained significant popular support in the Burundian countryside following the attempted coup in 1993.

The concept and the term regroupment (from the French, *regroupement*) derive most immediately from the French counterinsurgency doctrine developed in the 1950s. A historian of the Algerian independence war described the policy in terms that could well describe the current program in Burundi:

> In specified areas French soldiers systematically destroyed the small villages, forcing the citizens to settle in new villages or regroupment centers. The purpose of the regroupment policy was to remove whole populations from any contact with the nationalists. In some instances, it should be noted, the villagers volunteered to enter the regroupment centers after requesting protection from the French authorities against the exactions of the rebels. Such protection was often extended on condition that a given community resettle closer to a military establishment. More often than not, however, coercion was used...Once a regroupment had been accomplished, anyone found in the abandoned settlement was presumed guilty of rebel connections and was liable to be shot on sight.[46]

The governor of Karuzi, Lt. Col. Gabriel Gunungu, ordered the creation of Burundi's first regroupment camps in his province in February 1996, then expanded the program over the next several months to include most communes in the province. The Buyoya regime expanded the program following the July 1996 coup, organizing new regroupment camps in the provinces of Kayanza, Muramvya, Bubanza, Cibitoke, Bururi, and Bujumbura-Rural between August 1996 and February 1997. According to the government's own estimates, more than 300,000 people were living in regroupment camps in July 1997,[47] and even after many

---

[46]Alf Andrew Heggoy, *Insurgency and Counterinsurgency in Algeria* (Bloomington: Indiana University Press, 1972), p. 183. Heggoy (p. 214) cites official documents which put the number of people relocated into regroupment camps in Algeria by mid-April 1959 at over one million. For a discussion of forced displacement as a strategy in counterinsurgency operations, see Michael McClintock, *Instruments of Statecraft: U.S. Guerrilla Warfare, Counter-insurgency, and Counter-terrorism, 1940-1990* (New York: Pantheon Books, 1992). In chapter 11, McClintock discusses population control measures undertaken with U.S. support in South Vietnam and Guatemala.

[47]Minister of the Interior and Public Security, Colonel Epitace Bayaganakandi, Human Rights Watch interview in Bujumbura, July 3, 1997.

camps were subsequently closed in Kayanza and Muramvya, the U.N. Department of Humanitarian Affairs estimated that 570,000 people, or around 10 percent of Burundi's population, were living in camps, including more than 220,000 people in regroupment camps. NGO sources reported that new regroupment camps were being created in Bururi and Makamba in late 1997.[48]

The conflict in Burundi is an internal armed conflict and is regulated by the laws of war as defined in optional Protocol II of the Geneva Conventions of 1949. Article 17 of Protocol II prohibits the forced movement of civilians in all but strictly limited circumstances: "The displacement of the civilian population shall not be ordered for reasons related to the conflict unless the security of the civilians involved or imperative military reasons so demand."[49] Protections under human rights law also remain in force; rights that can never be derogated or suspended, under Article 4 (2) of the International Covenant on Civil and Political Rights, include: the right not to be arbitrarily deprived of one's life (Article 6); the right not to subjected to torture or cruel, inhuman or degrading treatment (Article 7); the right not to be held in slavery or servitude (Articles 8 (1) and 8 (2)); the right to be recognized as a person before the law (Article 16); and the right to freedom of thought, conscience, and religion (Article 18).

Burundian government and military officials have offered a variety of arguments in an attempt to justify regroupment under the obligations imposed by Protocol II and other treaties. Some officials have denied that regroupment camps exist distinct from other camps for the internally displaced, claiming that people have voluntarily gathered in camps for their own protection and that all camps were created to deal with displaced persons only. In an interview, the Minister of the Interior and Public Security, Col. Epitace Bayaganakandi, initially denied that the military had forced Hutu civilians into regroupment camps, claiming that the camps had been created at the request of the population: "The government never incited people to regroup. It was the population that asked the armed forces to give them

---

[48]U.N. Department of Humanitarian Affairs, Integrated Regional Information Network, "Emergency Update on the Great Lakes," October 28, 1997; personal communication, December 16, 1997.

[49]Article 17, Protocol Additional to the Geneva Conventions of 12 August 1949, and Relating to the Protection of Victims of Non-International Armed Conflicts (Protocol II), of 8 June 1977. Burundi succeeded to the four Geneva Conventions on December 1971 when it accepted the ratification by the former colonial power, Belgium. Burundi is also party to additional Protocols I and II to the Geneva Conventions and is a party to the International Covenant on Civil and Political Rights.

protection."[50]   The Minister of Communications Pierre-Claver Ndayicariye has similarly claimed that regroupment occurred not because of government orders but spontaneously as the population sought protection from the FDD.[51]   One person interviewed said, "People talk about regroupment as something new. But it is not new. This has been going on since 1993. When there is a war, you have to protect people, you have to protect the women and children."[52]

Testimonies gathered by Human Rights Watch clearly refute the claim that people gathered at regroupment camps voluntarily. Although according to the U.N. Special Rapporteur for Burundi some people did willingly move into camps when ordered to do so,[53] witnesses who spoke to Human Rights Watch emphasized that they had been driven from their homes by a campaign of sheer terror. People living in the camps reported that the military forced them into the camps against their will, threatening them with torture (including rape) or death if they refused, and pillaging, burning, and destroying their homes.   They insisted that people remain in the camps only because they are coerced to do so. One man interviewed in Karuzi reported that his family went to the camp at Bugenyuzi in September 1996. "We went because of the insecurity in the hills. The authorities came to encourage us to go into the camps. If we resisted, we were killed."[54] A man interviewed near Nyarurama Camp in Kayanza claimed that in his area the armed forces attacked people beginning in December 1996 to force them into the camps. "We were burned out of our homes.... We were pursued by the soldiers. They did not want us ιo stay on our hills. They killed many people.... The soldiers surrounded us and put us in the camp."[55] A man in Rutegama, Muramvya, said

---

[50]Human Rights Watch interview in Bujumbura with Col. Epitace Bayaganakandi, Minister of the Interior and Public Security, July 3, 1997.

[51]United Nations Department of Humanitarian Affairs, "Burundi: Humanitarian Situation Report, July 16-July 23."

[52]Human Rights Watch interview in Bujumbura, June 6, 1997.

[53]Paulo Sergio Pinheiro, Interim Report on the Human Rights Situation in Burundi Submitted by the Special Rapporteur of the Commission on Human Rights, Pursuant to Economic and Social Council Decision 1997/280 (NewYork: United Nations, October 7, 1997), A/52/505, p.13.

[54]Human Rights Watch interview near Bugenyuzi, Karuzi, June 13, 1997.

[55]Human Rights Watch interview in Buteganzwa, Kayanza, June 23, 1997.

"Soldiers created the camps. When they suspected that there was an area where the rebels were active, soldiers would come and order people to gather at a specific site. They killed anyone who refused."[56] These testimonies were corroborated by local and expatriate religious, health, and relief workers.

While houses are often completely destroyed, the quickest way to make them uninhabitable is by burning the roof off, as here at a village between Makamba and Vugizo.

Some military and political officials admitted that the armed forces had forced civilians into regroupment camps against their will, but they claimed that regroupment was carried out "for the security of civilians," as allowed in Protocol II of the Geneva Conventions. According to these officials, camps were created to protect the population, either from abuse by the FDD or from the danger of being mistaken for FDD soldiers and accidentally targeted by government troops. President Buyoya himself made a such an assertion in a recent *New York Times* interview, claiming, "We are obliged to regroup people to protect them.... We have to put them somewhere where they can live together in security."[57] The chief counselor to the governor of Kayanza told us that people "were regrouped for their own protection, in September and October. It was to be able to separate the

---

[56]Human Rights Watch interview in Rutegama, Muramvya, June 11, 1997.

[57]Quoted in James C. McKinley, "Hutu Families Pay Price in Burundi's Crackdown Against Guerrillas," *New York Times*, August 12, 1997.

innocent from those who are against order."[58] A soldier who was a guard at one of the camps in Kayanza said, "Before the camp, it was hard to tell the civilians from the rebels. The rebels would just throw down their arms. Then they looked like any other civilians, and we would arrive and be embarrassed."[59] According to Commandant Gabriel Bunyundo, the assistant to the governor of Karuzi,

> The assailants were active among the population.... The assailants demanded food, money, meat. The people were basically hostage ... At a certain time, there were many innocent people killed. When the assailants fled, they were followed by a part of the population. When the soldiers attacked, many of these people were killed. At a certain time, we said that people who believed themselves innocent should assemble themselves here and here and here, where there are military posts. After that, we pursued those who had arms and refused to disarm.[60]

The extensive use of violence to drive people into the camps and the large number of people deliberately killed and injured by soldiers within the camps demonstrates that "the security of civilians" was not the primary concern of the authorities. A substantial number of unarmed civilians were killed during the process of regroupment. In each of the provinces, after ordering the local population to regroup, the armed forces of Burundi carried out cleanup operations in which they shot, bayonetted, or stabbed unarmed men, women, and children who remained outside the camps. Once Hutu civilians were gathered in the camps, the soldiers arrested and summarily executed people they suspected of having ties to the CNDD. One health worker who served in an area where regroupment camps were being created observed that many of the hundreds of people he treated for gunshot wounds and other injuries during the formation of the camps came not from the countryside but from within the camps, where soldiers continued to terrorize the population and to search out people they suspected of supporting the FDD.[61]

---

[58]Human Rights Watch interview in Kayanza, June 23, 1997.

[59]Human Rights Watch interview in Butaganzwa, Kayanza, June 23, 1997.

[60]Human Rights Watch interview in Karuzi, June 13, 1997.

[61] Human Rights Watch interview, June 1997.

A third line of argument admits that regroupment was a military strategy but attempts to justify regroupment as necessary for the "imperative military reasons" allowed under Protocol II.[62] The army spokesperson, Colonel Isaie Nibizi, admitted that regroupment was undertaken for strategic purposes. "Regroupment is a military strategy decided on the national level.... The only issue is security."[63] After the attempted coup in 1993, the CNDD apparently made significant inroads in the countryside. The FDD received logistical support from civilians, and supporters of the CNDD organized parallel political structures, particularly in the area between the Kibira National Forest and Ruvubu National Park, including the provinces of Karuzi, Muramvya, Ngozi, Gitega, Kayanza, and Bubanza, which was a major corridor for FDD troop movement.[64] Regroupment was designed to isolate the FDD, to limit the ability of Hutu in rural areas to offer support to the FDD and other Hutu rebel groups, and to bring the rural Hutu population under the strict scrutiny and control of the military..

International legal experts, however, understand the "imperative military reasons" allowed under Protocol II in a limited sense to mean the removal of civilians from an expected site of direct combat. This phrase does not authorize indefinite detention of civilians in areas where support for an enemy exists, as in Burundi's regroupment policy. Military necessity may allow for the removal of civilians from an expected battlefield, but cannot be invoked as an excuse to gain military advantage by depopulating entire villages and holding the population hostage against their will in squalid conditions. The International Committee of the Red Cross (ICRC) adopts a similar position in its authoritative commentaries on the Geneva Protocols:

---

[62] Article 17, Protocol Additional to the Geneva Conventions of 12 August 1949, and Relating to the Protection of Victims of Non-International Armed Conflicts (Protocol II), of 8 June 1977.

[63] Human Rights Watch interview with Colonel Isaie Nibizi, Bujumbura, June 17, 1997.

[64] Government officials claimed that CNDD activity was extensive in the areas targeted for regroupment, and many civilians we interviewed confirmed that this was in fact the case.

Clearly, imperative military reasons cannot be justified by political motives. For example, *it would be prohibited to move a population in order to exercise more effective control over a dissident ethnic group.*[65]

The process of regroupment involved blatant disregard for the basic human rights of the civilian population, including their right to life, liberty and security of the person as stated in Article 3 of the Universal Declaration on Human Rights. The numerous executions that the military carried out inside the camps were violations of both the laws of war and human rights law.

The Burundian military created regroupment camps in areas where they believed that Hutu civilians were supporting the FDD, but they did not follow any selective process to determine who should be detained in the camps: ethnicity was the single determining factor. The military considered all Hutu in areas of FDD activity rebels or rebel sympathizers, and condemned them to live in the camps. Many people in the regroupment camps told Human Rights Watch that they consider themselves "prisoners" or "hostages," and indeed, people in the camps are not at liberty to return to their homes or travel freely. The regroupment camps thus essentially represent a collective punishment against the Hutu population. Article 4(2) of Protocol II clearly and unequivocally states that collective punishment "shall remain prohibited at any time and at any place whatsoever."[66]

Human Rights Abuses During the Formation of the Regroupment Camps

The Use of Mass Terror and Targeting of the Civilian Population
Burundi is flagrantly violating the rules of war and its obligations under human rights law by employing its armed forces to kill unarmed civilians, to rape women and girls, to pillage and destroy property, and to forcibly displace noncombatant men, women, and children. Article 4 of Protocol II to the Geneva Conventions declares that "All persons who do not take a direct part or who have ceased to take part in hostilities ... are entitled to respect for their person." Article 4 prohibits

---

[65] International Committee of the Red Cross, Commentary on the Additional Protocols of 8 June 1977 to the Geneva Conventions of 12 August 1949 (1987) at para 4854, p. 1473 (emphasis added).

[66] Art. 4(2)(b), Protocol II to the Geneva Conventions of 12 August 1949. The protections contained in Article 4 are listed as "fundamental guarantees." As the ICRC commentary comments, "The prohibitions are explicit and do not allow for any exception ... They are absolute obligations." ICRC, Commentary, para 4528, p. 1372.

"violence to the life, health and physical or mental well-being of persons" and specifically forbids pillage and rape.[67] According to Article 13(2) of Protocol II,

> The civilian population as such, as well as individual civilians, shall not be the object of attack. Acts or threats of violence the primary purpose of which is to spread terror among the civilian population are prohibited.[68]

Despite these clear prohibitions on the targeting of civilians during internal armed conflicts, the Burundian military is actively waging war against its own civilian population of Hutu origin through an orchestrated campaign of terror.

Witnesses interviewed for this report make clear that during regroupment the armed forces of Burundi attacked civilians without regard for their status as civilians or combatants. According to witnesses and to religious and health workers who worked in regroupment areas, in nearly all cases, those killed were unarmed and were not taking direct part in hostilities. The victims included many civilian women, children, and elderly, whose noncombatant status was readily apparent. Soldiers killed victims in their homes or in the forests and marshes where they were seeking refuge from attacks. A witness from Bugenyzui Commune in Karuzi testifies, "When the soldiers came, they killed anyone they saw."[69] The rape, looting and destruction of property which accompanied these campaigns are also egregious violations of international human rights and humanitarian law.

The process of forcing the civilian population into the regroupment camps during their formation involved extensive violence in all of the provinces where the military created camps.[70] In each of the provinces with extensive FDD activity,

---

[67]Article 4, Protocol II to the Geneva Conventions of 12 August 1949.

[68]Article 13(2), Protocol II to the Geneva Conventions of 12 August 1949. Article 13(3) states that "[c]ivilians shall enjoy the protection afforded by this Part, unless and for such time as they take a direct part in hostilities."

[69]Human Rights Watch interview in Bugenyuzi, Karuzi, June 13, 1997.

[70]The actual organization and function of the camps varies from one location to the next. For example, in Karuzi, Bubanza, and Kayanza, camps are organized by small villages, with most public activities taking place in the camps, while in Muramvya, the camps today are little more than a place to sleep. In Bururi, people have been gathered in towns, many of them living with local families and only a small number living in temporary housing.

military and political officials first ordered the population to assemble at designated sites, generally at military posts. Anyone who refused to assemble within a specified period of time, usually two days, would be considered a CNDD agent and therefore treated as a legitimate military target. Acutely aware of the history of military oppression and the military's past involvement in massacres, the majority of the population in many areas refused to assemble at the designated military posts. A man who had objected to the formation of regroupment camps in his home area in Bururi explained, "If we do that [enter regroupment camps], we become hostages."[71] As an example, according to one source, in Rutegama, Muramvya, only 7,000 people showed up at one designated camp site out of a population of 17,000, only 200 people out of 15,000 at a second site, and only forty people out of a population of 10,000 at a third.[72] Since the Burundian government created regroupment camps at the same time that refugee camps for Rwandan and Burundian Hutu were being closed in Eastern Zaire and Tanzania, the targeted population was not able to take refuge outside the country but instead attempted to hide from soldiers in their fields or in marshes and forests. Others simply stayed in their homes, hoping the military would leave them in peace.

Following the designated deadline for assembling in a camp, the military carried out *nettoyage*, cleanup operations, in which they systematically swept the hillsides, pillaging, burning and destroying homes, and capturing or killing anyone they encountered. As the *Economist* reported in December 1996, in areas where camps were created, "The emptied land has become a free-fire zone for the army. Its spokesman admitted as much last week, saying that anyone who had not moved into the new settlements would be treated as a rebel."[73]

Summary Executions of Civilians

The exact number of civilians that the armed forces killed while forming the camps is difficult to estimate. Since a number of camp residents interviewed had themselves initially refused to be regrouped and came to the camps only because they were captured by soldiers and escorted into the camps at gunpoint, it is clear that soldiers did not kill all persons they encountered in their homes or in the forests, fields, and marshes where they had fled rather than entering the camps. At the same time, however, testimonies make clear that soldiers shot or bayoneted

---

[71]Human Rights Watch interview in Bururi, June 21, 1997.

[72]Human Rights Watch interview in Bujumbura, June 6, 1997.

[73]*The Economist* (London), December 14, 1996, pp. 43-44.

hundreds, probably thousands of unarmed civilians who resisted regroupment. As noted, soldiers also arrested and summarily executed numerous civilians once they were inside the camps, accusing them of working with the FDD.

Human Rights Watch visited regroupment camps in Karuzi, Kayanza, Muramvya, Bubanza, and Bururi. In each of these provinces, witnesses testified that the armed forces were responsible for widespread summary executions and destruction of property during the creation of the camps. In the northern provinces of Karuzi, Kayanza, Bubanza, and Muramvya virtually every person interviewed in and around the camps reported that they had lost members of their immediate family during the creation of the camps.

For example, in Bihemba Regroupment Camp in Karuzi one middle-aged woman told us, "When the soldiers came, I ran, but they shot at us." When asked if anyone in her family had been killed during the formation of the regroupment camps, she reported that soldiers had killed her married son in August 1996 at Muyogoro, and another unmarried son in September at Bugenyuzi.[74] A man who lived nearby reported that he had lost his brother, age twenty-two, in August 1996, along with the brother's one-and-a-half-year-old son. In December, his brother-in-law, age twenty-nine, was imprisoned for two weeks before being killed. According to the witness, "At that time they took no matter who and imprisoned them."[75] Another man claimed that soldiers killed twelve people in his family, including one son, a brother and his three children, two sisters-in-law, a cousin, and others.[76]

The responses were similar wherever we conducted interviews. A witness from Mushikamo in Rutegama Commune of Muramvya reported that "The soldiers set up a position and assembled the population. They burned houses, stole livestock. They killed many people."[77] Another witness added, "The soldiers arrived and told people to come, and the people came. And those who did not were killed."[78] A man interviewed near Bugenyuzi camp in Karuzi reported that soldiers had killed his twenty-year-old cousin in February 1996, when the camps were first being

---

[74]Human Rights Watch interview at Bihemba, Karuzi, June 13, 1997.

[75]Human Rights Watch interview at Bihemba, Karuzi, June 13, 1997.

[76]Ibid.

[77]Human Rights Watch interview at Mushikamo, Rutegama, Muramvya, June 11, 1997.

[78]Ibid.

created, then later they killed two nephews, ages sixteen and fifteen, and his own three-year-old child. Since moving into the camp, he had lost a second child to illness.[79] A man interviewed near Buraniro Regroupment Camp in Buteganzwa, Kayanza, lost his sixty-five-year-old mother-in-law and his sister's three children.[80]

In a number of cases in Karuzi, Bubanza, and Muramvya, as the Human Rights Watch team was conducting interviews, a small crowd gathered, and people lined up to report members of their families who had been killed either where they were hiding outside the camps or once they entered the camps—children, sisters and brothers, parents and grandparents, uncles and aunts, cousins, husbands and wives. One man from Mpira Sector of Rutegama in Muramvya said that the military killed his father, Butahanze, age sixty, in 1993, then they killed his mother, Banhua, age forty-five, in June 1996. When asked to name relatives killed since the beginning of regroupment, he responded "Where can one begin? There were many, many. Too many to count. They [the armed forces] attacked the whole hill."[81]

No organized effort has been undertaken to determine how many people died overall during the formation of regroupment camps. Sources in Bururi said that in November 1996 soldiers killed fifty civilians who resisted regroupment at Mudende in Buyengero Commune.[82] A group calling itself "Christians of Ntara, Kayanza" lists the names, ages, and burial sites of eighty-four people killed by the military between December 2, 1996, and February 15, 1997, in Ninga Zone, Butaganzwa Commune, Kayanza.[83] Agence France Presse reported in mid-January that both an official of the Catholic diocese of Ngozi and a CNDD spokesperson claimed that the military had killed over 3,000 civilians in Kayanza in December and January.[84] Another anonymous document names 122 people killed by soldiers

---

[79]Human Rights Watch interview near Bugenyuzi, Karuzi, June 13, 1997.

[80]Human Rights Watch interview at Musema, Kayanza, June 23, 1997.

[81]Human Rights Watch interview in Rutegama, Muramvya, June 11, 1997.

[82]Human Rights Watch interview in Bururi, June 21, 1997.

[83]Abakristu bo mu Ntara ya Kayanza, "Urutonde rw'amazina y'abanyagihugu bamwe bamaze kugandagurwa n'igisoda c'uburundi muri Commune Butaganzwa—Zone Ninga."

[84]Cited in United Nations Department of Humanitarian Affairs, Integrated Regional Information Network, "Emergency Update on the Great Lakes," no. 82, January 20, 1997, and United Nations Department of Humanitarian Affairs, "U.N. Humanitarian Situation

in January and February 1997 on the hills Nyarunazi, Nyakararo, and Nyarukere in Rutegama Commune, Muramvya.[85] A group known as "SOS Genocide," claims that 538 people were killed in seven separate attacks in Rutegama between November 1996 and February 1997.[86] Church sources claim that government troops killed 400 civilians in the first week of January alone.[87] The main opposition party, Frodebu, estimates that "[i]n the eight months since the usurpation of power by Buyoya and the army, more than fifty thousand people have died, killed by the military under a single justification: the pursuit of rebels."[88]

Rape

In addition to killing hundreds of unarmed civilians, the armed forces of Burundi engaged in widespread rape of women and girls during the formation of the regroupment camps. Informants in Muramvya, Karuzi, Kayanza, and Bururi all reported incidents of rape by soldiers. Health workers in several provinces reported treating numerous women and girls who had been raped. One nurse described rape as a severe problem during the months in which the armed forces were attacking the population to drive them into the camps. When asked to estimate the numbers of women and girls raped during this period, she shook her head and said, "Many. Many, many. Too many to count."[89] A witness from Rutegama, Muramvya, reported that beginning in October 1996, "The soldiers

---

Report— Burundi (01/14-28), January 31, 1997.

[85] Anonymous untitled document provided to Human Rights Watch by sources in Bujumbura. The document ends with the note: "These people were killed during the human hunt for forced regroupment of the population. Numerous among the victims resisted and remained on their hills to cultivate their fields because of the planting season. Others who were too old hoped that the soldiers would leave them alone. This was a fatal error."

[86] SOS Genocide, "Special Cadeau fin d'Année," February 1997.

[87] United Nations Department of Humanitarian Affairs, "U.N. Humanitarian Situation Report—Burundi (01/14-28), January 31, 1997.

[88] Parti Sahwanya, Frodebu Secretariat General, "Memorandum sur la situation qui prevaut au Burundi: Avril 1997."

[89] Human Rights Watch interview, June 1997.

came and killed people. They raped women and then shot them. They burned houses, destroyed them, and stole all the goods inside as well as the livestock."[90]

The use of rape as a tactic of war is an especially grievous violation of international humanitarian law.[91] In the context of armed conflict, systematic rape is a particularly aggravated form of torture, and a breach of the most basic norms of humanitarian treatment. Human Rights Watch was able to document a consistent pattern of rape both during the military's campaign to force the population into the camps and later while persons were resident in the camps. There was no evidence troops were disciplined for rape, despite the widespread and notorious pattern of rape by military personnel, which strongly suggested that the military either condoned or encouraged the practice of rape. The brutality of the military's campaign, as evidenced by the frequent use of rape, torture and summary execution, further demonstrated that the military was little concerned with the safety of the civilian population while implementing the camp policy, despite official claims to the contrary.

Destruction of Homes

During regroupment, soldiers also destroyed thousands of homes and other buildings and looted the goods inside. In some cases, as in Burambi and Bugenyuzi Communes of Bururi, the soldiers forced people to burn their own homes before herding them into camps.[92] The military evidently undertook the destruction of houses to prevent those civilians ordered to regroup from returning to their homes and also to eliminate potential hiding places for FDD combatants.

The number of destroyed buildings whose ruins are visible when driving through Bubanza, Kayanza, Karuzi, Muramvya, and Bururi is astounding. In many rural areas, not a single building remains standing. Houses have not simply been burned, but walls have been demolished, so that nothing is left but piles of rubble. As one source said with irony, "We Burundians are specialists in building

---

[90]Human Rights Watch interview, Rutegama, Muramvya, June 11, 1997.

[91]For a detailed discussion of rape as an international crime during internal conflict, see Human Rights Watch and Fédération Internationale des Ligues des Droits de l'Homme, *Sexual Violence during the Rwandan Genocide and its Aftermath* (New York: Human Rights Watch, 1996).

[92]Human Rights Watch interviews in Bururi, June 21, 1997.

demolition."[93] One man from Mpira Sector of Rutegama in Muramvya testified that his home had been burned three times—once in 1993, again in June 1996, then again when camps were created in Muramvya in late 1996.[94] Many witnesses testified that before burning their homes, soldiers pillaged whatever they could carry that was of value. They burned other items, such as clothing and furniture. Witnesses repeatedly told us, "We have only the clothes that you see. Everything else was pillaged."

The tactics employed by the Burundian army in order to gain military advantage over the rebel insurgency directly target the largely Hutu civilian population. The devastation of an entire countryside is not a legitimate tactic of war, and has caused untold suffering among hundreds of thousands of civilians.

Human Rights and Conditions in the Regroupment Camps

Sanitary and Health Conditions in the Regroupment Camps

In creating the camps, the government of Burundi ignored its obligations to carry out adequate preparations to receive those forcibly displaced, as required under the exceptional cases authorized by Article 17 of Protocol II of the Geneva Conventions. "Should such displacements have to be carried out, all possible measures shall be taken in order that the civilian population may be received under satisfactory conditions of shelter, hygiene, health, safety and nutrition." The government and armed forces of Burundi clearly did not undertake "all possible measures" to accommodate the population they forcibly displaced. In most cases the government made no preparations at all for shelter, hygiene, health, and nutrition at the sites where they ordered the population to assemble. No advance preparations were made by the government or military for the provision of water or food in the camps. Because of the limited time allowed for assembling in the camps and the subsequent limitations on movement, civilians had to construct temporary housing out of whatever building materials were available in close proximity to the camps. No provisions were made for sewage, latrines, and other structures necessary for good hygiene. The military generally allowed only two days for the population to assemble, and sometimes as little as two hours, wholly inadequate for people to prepare.

Conditions in the regroupment camps have steadily deteriorated since their creation. The camps are cramped and overcrowded, housing is meager, and

---

[93]Human Rights Watch interview in Bujumbura, June 1997.

[94]Human Rights Watch interview in Rutegama, Muramvya, June 11, 1997.

facilities for water and waste disposal are grossly inadequate. Food supplies are also extremely scarce, in part because of the disruptions to food production resulting from regroupment. As a result, disease and malnutrition are rampant. In addition, although the armed forces had for a time stopped large-scale massacres, they continued to employ violence on a smaller scale, engaging in rape, torture, and extrajudicial executions. The armed forces regularly pillage from civilians in the camps, and in many locations they have instituted forced labor.

A typical regroupment camp in Karuzi. (This specific camp is Bihemba.)

Due to the crowded conditions in the camps and inadequate facilities for sanitation, disease is rampant in the camps. Camps ranged in size from several thousand people to more than 22,000, as at Bugenyuzi camp in Karuzi.[95] The

---

[95]According to statistics provided by the governor's office in Karuzi, a total of 139,682 people were living in twenty-two camps, the vast majority Hutu in forced regroupment camps, although this figure includes a small number of Tutsi in voluntary displacement camps. In mid-June, the largest regroupment camps in that province were Bugenyuzi with 22,289 residents, Ntunda with 16,646, Gihogazi with 14,960, Bihemba with 14,224, Mugogo with 13,339, Cantikiro with 10,407, Rusamazo with 9,574, and Miyogero with 9,105. In Kayanza, two camps visited by Human Rights Watch, Nyarurama and Buraniro, had respectively 15,000 and 16,000 residents (including approximately 3,000 displaced Tutsi in a separate section). The total number in the regroupment camps in Kayanza in June, 1997, was 76,000.

location for camps was determined by security concerns—they are generally located at existing military posts—without consideration of reliable supplies of fresh water and other requirements for health and hygiene. The military and the government have expended little effort to provide necessary facilities for the camps since their creation, even though Article 17(2) of Protocol II requires them to do so. As a result, epidemics of typhus, cholera, measles and other diseases have occurred in a number of the camps, as well as exaggerated levels of malaria, respiratory ailments, scabies, and other conditions related to overcrowding and bad hygiene. The World Health Organization reported a serious typhus epidemic in the camps in Kayanza, Karuzi, and Muramvya in March 1997, with 500 to 1,000 new cases reported daily.[96]

Health problems have been exacerbated by malnutrition, which is at chronic levels in some camps. In many areas, the armed forces now allow farmers to leave the camps to work in their fields during the day, provided they return to the camp by a specified time, usually 5 or 6 p.m. However, those who live far from the camps are not allowed to leave, for fear that they will not return,[97] and people in areas of ongoing insecurity, as in Bubanza, Cibitoke, and parts of Bururi, are likewise restricted to the camps. Even where people are now allowed to farm, food production had been halted for a number of months and continues to be disrupted. One aid worker told Human Rights Watch that on a recent visit to a camp in Karuzi he had seen a man carrying an immature bunch of bananas, "weeks before it would usually be harvested." When he asked why the man had harvested his bananas so early, he said that if he did not, they would be stolen from his fields. Because he and other camp residents did not live at home, they could not protect their crops from theft.[98]

As a result of these disruptions, food supplies in the camps are extremely limited, and malnutrition is endemic. A July report by the World Health Organization and the Food and Agriculture Organization concludes that food security has steadily deteriorated since 1993 and confirms widespread malnutrition

---

[96]United Nations Department of Humanitarian Affairs, Integrated Regional Information Network, "Emergency Update on the Great Lakes," no. 124, March 11, 1997.

[97]Some people in Karuzi normally reside as far as five hours from the camps where they are required to live. One man interviewed in Bugenyuzi as he was entering the camp reported that he had been hiking for more than six hours with a heavy sack of manioc which he had purchased at a market.

[98]Human Rights Watch interview in Gitega, June 12, 1997.

among both children and adults.[99]   The worst cases of malnutrition can be witnessed in Bubanza and Cibitoke, where ongoing fighting continues to prevent farmers from working their fields, and in Karuzi, where regroupment camps have been in place for more than a year. In these locations, we saw numerous signs of severe malnutrition in both children and adults—bloating of the legs and belly, hair straightened and bleached white. Some victims of malnutrition were so weak that they required a support to walk, while others could not walk at all.[100] As one health worker said, "Child malnutrition is not unusual, but when you have adult malnutrition, you know the situation is serious."[101]

Malnutrition and illness combine to create high levels of mortality in the camps. Health workers report much higher than normal numbers of patients, despite difficulties accessing health centers because of restrictions on movement, and higher than normal rates of death. Many camp residents reported that since entering the camps they had lost members of their family to disease or starvation—children but also many adults. According to one foreign religious worker familiar with the regroupment camps, "It is more true to say that they are extermination camps. All that is lacking is the gas chamber. You watch as members of the family slowly die off, one by one, from tuberculosis, malaria, dysentery, starvation."[102] The main opposition party Frodebu characterizes the regroupment camps as "concentration camps."[103]

The government has attempted to blame the international community for the dire conditions in the regroupment camps. In late 1996, the Buyoya regime announced to the international community that it needed assistance in establishing regroupment camps—building supplies, water and sanitation facilities, and food. Foreign governments and international nongovernmental organizations refused to provide the assistance, claiming (based in part on observation of existing camps in

---

[99]Cited in United Nations Department of Humanitarian Affairs, Integrated Regional Information Network, "Weekly Roundup," no. 15-97, July 28-August 4, 1997.

[100]Human Rights Watch investigations in Bubanza, June 10 and 27, 1997, and Karuzi, June 13, 1997.

[101]Human Rights Watch interview, June 1997.

[102]Human Rights Watch interview in Bujumbura, June 10, 1997.

[103]See Parti Sahwanya Frodebu, Secretariat General, "Memorandum sur la situation qui prevaut au Burundi: Avril 1997."

Karuzi) that forced regroupment was a violation of humanitarian law and that the creation of camps was a military strategy which the international community had no business supporting. The government then restricted access to areas where they planned to establish camps and, several months later when the camps were in place, again called on the international community to provide assistance, a request which was again denied.[104]

The issue of assistance to regroupment camps has presented an ethical quandary for foreign governments, multilateral organizations, and NGOs. The humanitarian problems resulting from the camps are serious, but the governments and relief organizations do not want to intervene in the camps in a way that contributes to the regroupment policy, which they regard as a military strategy. Martin Griffiths, the United Nations Regional Humanitarian Coordinator for the Great Lakes, explained in March 1997 that humanitarian agencies, "face the dilemma of how to meet the needs of those in the camp without having the effect of encouraging or supporting the military policy."[105] The regroupment camps have been established for the express purpose of concentrating, controlling, and culling a civilian population distinguished solely by its ethnicity: this program of forced regroupment represents a violation of the rules of war.

Summary Executions, Torture, Rape and other abuses in the Regroupment Camps

In addition to creating a humanitarian catastrophe by forcing the Hutu population into the camps, the armed forces who oversee the camps continue to engage in numerous killings, rape, torture, and theft. In the areas of Kayanza, Karuzi, and Muramvya where regroupment camps exist, the armed forces do not now engage in indiscriminate attacks on the civilian population as they did while they were attempting to force people out of hiding and into the camps, since the entire population now lives in the camps, and the military thoroughly controls the countryside. However, the armed forces continue to use violence in the camps selectively. They engage in torture, extrajudicial executions, and "disappearances," generally targeting people who challenge their authority or cause other problems and whose punishment can serve as examples to others in the camps. A number of Hutu pointed out the similarities between the current violence in the camps and the "selective genocide" in 1972. As one Hutu leader commented:

---

[104]Human Rights Watch interviews, Bujumbura, June 9 and 17, 1997.

[105]Cited in United Nations Department of Humanitarian Affairs, Integrated Regional Information Network, "Emergency Update on the Great Lakes," no. 121, March 9, 1997.

In the regroupment camps, they kill the most intelligent first—teachers, catechists, small business people, those who can make commentary. It is the same as in 1972. In these regions, they no longer go to school.[106]

According to the governor of Kayanza, the government has used the regroupment camps to dissuade the population from supporting the FDD and convince them to work with the government. According to the governor, the population was "intoxicated" by the propaganda of the FDD. In the camps, "there has been re-education of those who worked with the armed bands, a detoxification of the population. ... They have to put themselves on the right path. Ninety percent are already on the right path. The population and the forces of order are working together."[107] The commandant of Nyarurama Camp echoed a similar sentiment. "The population needs to be resensitized, reeducated, because they have been led down a bad path. What we are doing here is reeducating the population."[108]

Investigations by Human Rights Watch, however, indicate that the main lesson that the armed forces have taught camp residents is fear. Residents of Nyarurama and Buraniro Camps reported to Human Rights Watch that soldiers regularly arrest and torture individuals. One older woman interviewed near Nyarurama Camp described how every day women and men in the camp are taken to the military post and tortured. She demonstrated how people are laid down on their stomachs and beaten with a stick on the back, around the kidneys, and on the buttocks. People are beaten if they return late from their fields, if they violate camp policy, or if they simply irritate the camp guards. "If you speak a way they don't like, if you laugh, they arrest you," the woman reported. The woman said that one of her sons was recently taken by the guards and beaten.[109] Other witnesses corroborated her

---

[106]Human Rights Watch interview, June 1997.

[107]Human Rights Watch interview with Colonel Daniel Nengeri, governor of Kayanza, in Kayanza, June 24, 1997.

[108]Human Rights Watch interview, at Nyarurama, Kayanza, June 23, 1997. McClintock, op. cit., writes that the French used regroupment in Algeria as part of a program of psychological warfare that had four goals: "counter the effect of enemy propaganda on their own forces; attack the enemy's political network; aid in the destruction of enemy forces; and, most extraordinary, to organize and reeducate the suspect population as a whole" (p. 261). The goals of regroupment in Burundi follow this model.

[109]Human Rights Watch interview near Nyarurama, Kayanza, June 23, 1997.

assertions about the prevalence of beatings by the armed forces. According to the witnesses, the beating is sometimes of a severity great enough to lead to permanent injury or death. The process of "reeducation" in the camps in Kayanza apparently involves instilling fear in the population and teaching obedience through violence.

Young boys in regroupment camps like this one become familiar with being surrounded by loaded semi-automatic machine guns.

Beating and torture are practiced in camps in other provinces as well. Witnesses in Bihemba and Bugenyuzi Camps in Karuzi reported that soldiers regularly beat people in those camps. According to one witness at Bugenyuzi, "Soldiers come through every night and beat people and demand beers and girls."[110] In Muramvya, witnesses reported that all men are required to participate in nightly patrols. Those who fail to participate are fined and beaten.[111]

In addition to beatings and torture, witnesses reported regular summary executions, "disappearances," and arbitrary detentions in the camps. A witness from Rumonge in Bururi testified that "If the soldiers encounter someone they don't know, they kill them immediately."[112] The older woman from Nyarurama

---

[110]Human Rights Watch interview, in Karuzi, June 13, 1997.

[111]Human Rights Watch interview at Mpira Sector, Rutegama Commune, Muramvya, June 11, 1997.

[112]Human Rights Watch interview at Kizuka, Bururi, July 1, 1997.

whose testimony about torture is cited above reported that another of her sons, a thirty-five-year-old married father of two, "disappeared" in January 1997 and was presumed dead. She had spoken with authorities who claimed that he must have fled to join the rebels, "But I know that he would not flee and leave his wife and two small children."[113] One man from Nyarurama Camp in Kayanza reported that the number of executions and "disappearances" at that camp had declined since March, "But they still beat people. They even imprisoned me for a week, just last week. There were trees cut, and someone accused me. I was arrested and beaten badly the first day [of my detention]."[114] A fifty-eight-year-old grandmother from Nyarurama told a *Guardian* reporter, "They made us come here. ... They tell us it is for our own good, but they do not treat us well. They beat us and they kill people."[115] Witnesses from Bihemba and Bugenyuzi in Karuzi similarly reported that soldiers kill people less frequently than they did in 1996 and early 1997 when they were creating the camps and culling out suspected FDD operatives and community leaders, but they continue to arbitrarily arrest people, and sometimes those imprisoned "disappear." One young man at Bihemba Camp reported that groups of Tutsi from one of Karuzi's three camps for the displaced periodically come to the camps accompanied by a few soldiers. They take away people they suspect of involvement in local attacks on Tutsi following Ndadaye's death in 1993. Those taken, mostly young men, are never seen again and, according to the witness, are killed. According to the witness, "Every week they come to take people away."[116]

A witness from Buraniro Camp in Kayanza said that "disappearances" and summary executions continued at that camp. He gave the example of Léonce Nibarutu, a Hutu who was originally from Buteganzwa, where his brother was a councilor of Nyabibuye Zone. Nibarutu lived in Bujumbura, but at the beginning of June he had come back to Buteganzwa to visit his family. According to the witness, Nibarutu "had all of his papers [for identification and travel], but he crossed someone on the path who did not like him. This man contacted the soldiers, and they took him to the military camp, where they beat him all night. In

---

[113]Human Rights Watch interview near Nyarurama, Kayanza, June 23, 1997.

[114]Human Rights Watch interview near Nyarurama, Kayanza, June 23, 1997.

[115]Chris McGreal, "No Fences, but Hutus are in Prison," *The Guardian and Mail*, July 18, 1997.

[116]Human Rights Watch interview at Bihemba, Karuzi, June 13, 1997.

the morning he was dead."[117] The witness, who was a friend of the victim, was among those who buried the body and saw the evidence of death from torture.

Military and regroupment soldiers move by at dusk at the entrance to a regroupment camp.

Camp residents and other informants identified rape as a continuing problem in the regroupment camps. Although some witnesses in the camps were reluctant to discuss the topic of sexual violence because of serious social taboos which implicate the rape victim,[118] other witnesses reported that soldiers regularly rape women and girls. Health workers in several provinces reported encountering frequent cases of rape. According to their reports, while rape was most widespread during the formation of the camps, soldiers continue to rape women and girls on an almost daily basis. The armed forces seem to use sexual violence against women as one of the means to subdue the population, humiliating both the women and their families and contributing to a general atmosphere of fear. In addition,

---

[117]Human Rights Watch interview at Musema, Buteganzwa, Kayanza, July 23, 1997.

[118]In one case in Karuzi, when Human Rights Watch asked a group of men about rape in the camp, they first claimed that it was a problem in other camps but not theirs. They then claimed that it depended on the "weakness of the girls." Other witnesses, however, confirmed that rape was a serious problem.

according to some reports soldiers appear to view access to women as one of the spoils of their victory over the population.[119]

Forced Labor within the Regroupment Camps

The use of forced labor within the camps is a widespread practice. Sources from the regroupment camps in Karuzi claimed that soldiers require them to carry water, provide food, and make charcoal for them, a highly labor intensive process. If they do not provide these services, they are beaten or arrested. People complained that, although they are themselves starving, what little they are able to harvest from their fields is taken from them by soldiers.[120] According to Léonce Ngendakumana, the president of the National Assembly and a Hutu from Frodebu, "People are being used like slaves. They have to work for the soldiers and others. They harvest crops, but they cannot keep the harvests for themselves."[121]

Ongoing Developments in Regroupment Policy

From the perspective of the Buyoya regime, regroupment camps have been an extremely successful military strategy. Numerous people interviewed by Human Rights Watch confirmed government claims that the FDD was active in the countryside prior to the formation of the camps and that the creation of the camps and the related violence had, in some regions, including most of Kayanza, Karuzi, and Muramvya, almost entirely subdued the population and driven out the FDD, at least for the time being. An informant in Rutegama, Muramvya reported that the FDD was very active in the area before regroupment. They had organized a parallel administration and received logistical support from the population. "But they are all gone. They were driven out of this area."[122] Informants in Karuzi and Kayanza testified similarly that the FDD had been active in their region but that they were no longer present.

While the regroupment camps have served the short term military and strategic interests of the government, it is not accurate to claim, as did some government and military officials, that the population is more secure. As one man at Bihemba Camp in Karuzi said, "I cannot say there is security here, because we are like

---

[119]Human Rights Watch interviews in Karuzi and Kayanza, June 1997.

[120]Human Rights Watch interviews, Karuzi, June 13, 1997.

[121]Human Rights Watch interview, Bujumbura, June 17, 1997.

[122]Human Rights Watch interview, Rutegama, Muramvya, June 11, 1997.

prisoners here. We are hostages."[123] The population is being held in the camps against their will, and they continue to suffer from arbitrary detentions and extrajudicial executions, rape, pillage, and malnutrition and disease. The people in the camps express growing frustration and anger at their continued internment. A group of witnesses in Bihemba Camp complained vociferously, "The authorities do not let us go home. There was insecurity before, but now there is no longer a problem [with the FDD], so we should be able to go home."[124]

The camps remain a major diplomatic liability for the Buyoya regime. The continuation of a policy that denies liberty to several hundred thousand people and encourages other human rights abuses undermines government efforts to appear moderate and to attain a renewal of bilateral aid and an end to sanctions. The United States embassy has taken a clear position in opposition to the regroupment camps, and both the U.S. Agency for International Development (USAID) and the European Community Humanitarian Office (ECHO) have made aid contingent on elimination of the camps.[125]

As a result of these pressures and the success of the policy in reducing FDD activity in certain areas, the government has made some moves to modify its regroupment policy. In Muramvya and Kayanza some camps have already been eliminated, and in Karuzi the government has begun moving the population into smaller camps closer to their homes. Unfortunately, while the changes in regroupment policy currently being implemented may address humanitarian concerns, such as access to food and potable water, they largely fail to address other ongoing human rights issues, because freedom of movement continues to be restricted and the population continues to be exposed to arbitrary detention, torture, and killing. Furthermore, the government has no plans to close regroupment camps in regions of continued FDD activity, such as Bubanza, and they have created new camps in Makamba and Bururi, where insurgent activity has increased.

The armed forces began creating regroupment camps in Rutegama commune of Muramvya, in October 1996, and continued to use extensive violence in the commune until February 1997, by which time they had eliminated the FDD presence from the area and the Hutu population had ended open signs of resistance. As early as February 1997, soldiers began to allow some of the population to leave the camp at Mushikamo. However, they did not allow the people simply to return

---

[123]Human Rights Watch interview, Bihemba, Karuzi, June 13, 1997.

[124]Human Rights Watch interview, Bihemba, Karuzi, June 13, 1997.

[125]See joint statement of USAID and ECHO of May 13, 1997.

to their homes. While people were allowed to rebuild their houses and can now work their fields during the day, at night soldiers continue to require the population to concentrate. The women and children from each hill (one of the divisions in the political structure) are required to gather in one home each night, while the men from each hill are organized into a group that patrols the area. Any woman or child who fails to show up at the designated site or man who fails to join in the patrols is beaten and fined and risks being identified as an FDD agent and killed. A similar situation prevails at Mpira Camp, where four large pavilions have been constructed to house the women and children at night, but where all other activities are carried out at home.[126]

In Kayanza, the governor announced plans in June 1997 to disband the regroupment camps within a period of several months. Under the plan, however, people were not going to be allowed to reconstruct their homes on their original locations, scattered about the hillsides according to Burundian custom. Instead, the government said it would organize the construction of new homes, grouped together along roads, where they could be "better protected" by the armed forces. According to the governor's office, various international and local nongovernmental organizations would assist in the construction, providing windows, doors, and roofing materials.[127]

People did in fact begin to leave camps in some communes of Kayanza in late August under a government-sponsored initiative in which those leaving the camps were provided assistance from the World Food Program and several NGOs. People were initially allowed to return to their homes, though the government began a campaign to construct houses along the roads to which it could potentially force people to relocate. Once the return organized by the government began, however, thousands of people began to leave the camps spontaneously, and the closure of the camps was suspended in late September, supposedly due to security concerns.[128]

---

[126]Human Rights Watch interviews in Muramvya, June 11, 1997.

[127]Human Rights Watch interviews with chief counselor and governor of Kayanza, in Kayanza, June 23 and 24, 1997.

[128]Catholic Relief Services, "Situation Report for Burundi/Rwanda/Uganda," September 1997; U.N. Department of Humanitarian Affairs, IRIN, "Emergency Update No. 234 on the Great Lakes," August 22, 1997; U.N. Department of Humanitarian Affairs, IRIN, "Emergency Update No. 245 on the Great Lakes," September 10, 1997; U.N. Department of Humanitarian Affairs, IRIN, "Emergency Update No. 245 on the Great Lakes," October 6, 1997.

In Karuzi, where regroupment camps have been in existence longest and health conditions are most degraded, the government has announced plans to decentralize the regroupment program.[129] The assistant to the governor told Human Rights Watch in June 1997 that the provincial government was planning to divide large camps, which contained as many as 22,000 people, into smaller camps "closer to the hills where people live."[130] In late November 1997, the governor of Karuzi pledged to dismantle the camps entirely by the end of the year and claimed that several thousand people had already been allowed to return to their homes. In fact, the armed forces were not allowing people to return to their homes but concentrating them in small camps along the main roads, as humanitarian sources reported to the U.N. Department of Humanitarian Affairs. The changes to the regroupment policy in Karuzi represent a decentralization, not an elimination, of the camps.[131]

The changes to regroupment policy in Muramvya, Kayanza, and Karuzi may help to alleviate humanitarian problems, but they will not eliminate the human rights violations inherent to the camps. In all three provinces, the government maintains that under its plan, people should have better housing and access to their fields, which should diminish the risk of disease and famine. However, the military will continue to keep the population under strict surveillance and control. The population will continue to be exposed to violations by the armed forces against their person and property and will continue to be denied basic freedoms, such as the freedom to reside where they wish. While all three proposals are designed to appease the international community, they represent merely an adjustment of the regroupment policy, not its elimination.

In the case of Muramvya, former residents of Mushikamo Camp told Human Rights Watch they were pleased that the camp had been closed several months earlier. As one community elder explained, "We were regrouped. We gathered on orders from the military. But there was no shelter for us. There were many dead in the camp. We wanted to leave because many were sick and hungry, and we

---

[129]Human Rights Watch interviews with NGO and diplomatic sources, June 1997.

[130]Human Rights Watch interview with Com. Bunyundo Gabriel, assistant to the governor of Karuzi, in Karuzi, June 13, 1997.

[131] U.N. Department of Humanitarian Affairs, IRIN, "Update No. 298 for Central and Eastern Africa," November 22-24, 1997; U.N. Department of Humanitarian Affairs, IRIN, "Weekly Round-up 27-97 of Main Events in the Great Lakes region, October 24, 1997; personal communication, December 1997.

would have died there."[132] Yet those interviewed made it clear that they continue to live in fear, because the military continues to monitor them closely and to restrict their freedom. The obligatory patrols for men allow the military to closely regulate their whereabouts, while soldiers continue to intimidate the population. While there is no longer a camp, per se, the human rights situation has not significantly improved, and people continue to be denied the right to live in their own homes.[133]

In the cases of Kayanza and Karuzi, both NGOs and diplomatic sources expressed concern that the plan to concentrate housing in villages along roads represented merely a decentralization of the camps. The military would continue to monitor and harass the population.[134] Obligatory nightly patrols for men already existed in Kayanza, and the governor made clear that this practice would continue.[135] The government's conduct in its reconstruction program raised concerns. While the governor and his assistant told Human Rights Watch that the government had already begun the construction of homes to prepare for camp closure, interviews in Rango, Muhanga, and Butaganzwa communes revealed that the homes under construction at that point were intended exclusively for displaced Tutsi, not for Hutu from regroupment camps.[136] While the government has a legitimate interest in building housing for anyone in need, the discrimination in rehabilitation programs appears to confirm the doubts about the government's real interests regarding the Hutu population.

The plans for dissolution of the camps in Kayanza, Karuzi, and Muramvya represent models that could potentially be applied to camps in Bubanza, Bururi, and elsewhere to improve Burundi's international image while maintaining strict control over the Hutu population. The international community must closely monitor whatever developments take place in the regroupment policy and, should the government of Burundi accept a closure of camps as an element in negotiations, must see that the camps are in fact closed and that the freedom of movement and other human rights are fully respected. The government of Burundi must also be monitored to ensure that it follows through on any planned closure, since

---

[132]Human Rights Watch interview at Mushikamo, Muramvya, June 11, 1997.

[133]Human Rights Watch interviews at Mushikamo, Muramvya, June 11, 1997.

[134]Human Rights Watch interviews in Bujumbura and Kayanza, June and July 1997.

[135]Human Rights Watch interview with Col. Daniel Nengeri in Kayanza, June 24, 1997.

[136]Human Rights Watch interviews in Kayanza, June 23 and 24, 1997.

government authorities told the United Nations Regional Humanitarian Coordinator for the Great Lakes in March 1997 that most camps would be closed by June, but Human Rights Watch found that by July only one camp had been closed.[137]

While the success of the regroupment policy in suppressing visible resistance by the Hutu population and quashing active support for the FDD has led the Buyoya regime to modify the program in Kayanza, Karuzi, and Muramvya, the regroupment policy has been continued or expanded in areas where the FDD continues to operate. In fact, even as camps in the north of Burundi are being dismantled or decentralized, new camps continue to be created in the south. Since the FDD launched a major campaign in Makamba and Bururi in April 1997, the Buyoya regime has forced thousands of people in these provinces and in parts of Bujumbura-Rural, into new regroupment camps. While interviews conducted in June and July 1997 indicated that the creation of these new camps initially involved less violence than in the earlier wave of camp creation, with the population generally obeying government and military instructions to assemble, subsequent camp creation in Bujumbura-Rural, Bururi, and Makamba has apparently been more forceful.

In Muhuta Commune, Bujumbura-Rural, the military forced the local Hutu population into camps following FDD attacks on three occasions. In November 1996, the commandant of the military camp in the area forced the population into a camp after the FDD ambushed a military truck on the Lake Tanganyika road. The military allowed people to go home in December, but then in February 1997 the military again forced people into the camps following the assassination of a local government official. This time the military officer who gave the order allowed people only two hours to assemble. Again authorities allowed the population to return home after a month. When the FDD established a military presence in the hills above Magara in May 1997, the military forced the population of the area into a camp at Rutundo for a third time, and this time the camp appears to be more permanent.[138]

In some communes of Makamba and Bururi, where the risk of retaliation by troops was apparent, the population voluntarily went to government assembly points when the FDD attacked the region in April and May 1997. Government officials in both provinces told Human Rights Watch that they had informed the

---

[137]United Nations Department of Humanitarian Affairs, Integrated Regional Information Network, "Emergency Update on the Great Lakes," no. 121, March 9, 1997.

[138]Human Rights Watch interviews in Bujumbura, June 26, 1997, and in Bujumbura-Rural, June 28, 1997.

population prior to the attacks where they should gather if an attack ever occurred, and when the attacks did take place, the population did as they had been told. The administrator of Makamba Commune told Human Rights Watch, "We were attacked last here [in the south], so we had a chance to prepare the population. We told people to flee together to military posts, where they could be protected."[139] Similarly, according to the governor of Bururi, "The two ethnicities fled together and remain together."[140]

Human Rights Watch interviews with people in these provinces confirmed that the majority of people had fled to camps voluntarily, however, in some cases those who resisted were forced into the camps or killed. The administrator of Vugizo Zone of Makamba told Human Rights Watch that the population had fled voluntarily into camps after the FDD attacked the commune in mid-April 1997. However, 800 people were "taken hostage" by the FDD, and the military went and "brought them back."[141] According to interviews with Hutu civilians in Vugizo, however, these people were not taken hostage but chose to flee into the bush rather than into the camps. The military did not rescue them from the FDD, as the administrator claimed, but forced them into the camps. A number of other Hutu went into the camps only because they were compelled to do so by the military.[142] The armed forces have offered similar stories of "freeing" people "held hostage" by the FDD in other regions. The armed forces claimed on November 9, 1997, that they had freed more than 2,000 people held hostage by the FDD in Cibitoke.[143]

When the FDD attacked Vugizo, Makamba, they looted homes, stealing cattle, food, and other items, and the population fled. Some people went voluntarily to designated camp sites, but many others went into the bush. During the next several weeks, the military sought out people in the bush and forced them into camps. According to one informant from Vugizo, "Around 8 p.m. at Karonge in Vugizo, they [the FDD] began to shoot and burn houses. People hid when the shooting

---

[139]Human Rights Watch interview in Mabanda, Makamba, June 18, 1997.

[140]Human Rights Watch interview with André Ndayizamba in Bururi, June 20, 1997.

[141]Human Rights Watch interview with Joseph Bahendozi in Vugizo, Makamba, June 19, 1997.

[142]Human Rights Watch interview in Vugizo, Makamba, June 19, 1997.

[143]"Radio Reports Security Forces Free Over 2,000," FBIS Daily Report, November 9, 1997,

began. Those who refused to take refuge were killed. The assailants [FDD] did not kill but burned buildings. Those who stayed at home were killed by the military."[144] Another man confirmed that soldiers killed his father at Mbizi. Apparently, however, the military forced most people who were hiding in the bush into the camps rather than killing them. In parts of Bururi, the military burned a large number of homes to drive Hutu into camps.[145]

Since Human Rights Watch visited Makamba and Bururi in June and July 1997, the armed forces have created a number of new regroupment camps in the communes of Buyengero and Burambi, Bururi, Nyanza-Lac and Mabanda, Makamba, and perhaps in other locations, including parts of Bujumbura-Rural. While some people may have voluntarily followed government orders to enter these new camps, humanitarian sources indicate that people resisted regroupment and the armed forces used considerable force.[146] Unfortunately because of insecurity in these areas, detailed information about the formation of the camps and their current conditions is unavailable.

In some cases, the armed forces have created regroupment camps only temporarily, in order to search for FDD combatants in the area and to ferret out their supporters. One source told Human Rights Watch, "At Buruhukiro, the governor wanted to do a nettoyage [clean-up operation], so they gave them ten minutes or a half hour to come to the center. They sent them back after one week."[147] It is unclear how many civilians were killed during the clean-up operation.

---

[144]Human Rights Watch interview in Vugizo, Makamba, June 19, 1997.

[145]Human Rights Watch interviews in Bururi, June 20 and 21, 1997.

[146]Personal communication, December 16, 1997.

[147]Human Rights Watch interview in Bururi, June 20, 1997.

IV. CONTINUING HUMAN RIGHTS VIOLATIONS
BY THE ARMED FORCES OF BURUNDI AND TUTSI MILITIA

The armed forces of Burundi have engaged in a wide range of human rights violations since the July 1996 coup, focused overwhelmingly on the Hutu civilian population. While the violations have generally been most severe in areas where the policy of regroupment has been implemented, the armed forces throughout the country have engaged in indiscriminate attacks on civilians, extrajudicial executions, rape, looting, and torture. Tutsi civilians, with backing from the military, have been involved in theft, "disappearances," and other abuses. The practice of forced labor has also been increasing.

Indiscriminate Attacks on Civilians

The Burundian armed forces have regularly killed and wounded civilians in zones of combat. In some cases, the armed forces have killed civilians during exchanges with the rebel Forces for the Defense of Democracy (FDD), or in indiscriminate attacks in which the distinction between civilians and combatants was disregarded. The army spokesman announced in December 1997 that the armed forces had launched a shoot-on-sight operation in Bujumbura-Rural. He claimed, "As soon as we locate them, we kill them." He went on, however, to admit the difficulty soldiers had in distinguishing between armed rebels and noncombatant civilians. "We can only identify them when they fire on us," he

An ad hoc cross is made from sticks for this victim of the military in Bujumbura-Rural.

said.[148]

However, according to numerous testimonies from both Burundian and expatriate sources, in numerous cases soldiers have not simply been mistaken but have intentionally targeted civilians for attack, generally in retaliation for FDD attacks, particularly when those attacks have resulted in military casualties. As one informant explains, "You never hear of direct battles. It is always the assailants coming down to steal, which they have to do to survive. Then the army comes in and attacks the population. They never get the rebels. They always kill the civilians."[149]

Since the civil war began in 1993, the armed forces have targeted civilians in most areas of FDD activity, including areas where regroupment camps were created, as discussed in chapter three, and in other areas, such as Bujumbura-Rural, Bubanza, and Cibitoke and, since April 1997, Makamba and Bururi. In speaking with Human Rights Watch, the governor of Bururi expressed the sentiment that may motivate military attacks on civilians:

> The assailants passed by Makamba and into Nyanda and Buyengero communes [of Bururi province]. When they came to Bururi commune, when the population saw them, they fled to the cities and to military posts. This was the case in Rutovu and Songa communes as well. Thus, soldiers could easily target rebels without targeting the local population.... The situation in Burambi and Buyengero was more complicated. There was a confusion. Where people fled, the military was not confused about who the rebels were. But in these sectors, the population did not go to the centers—Buyengero, Rumonge, Burambi, Muyange. There were problems there, because the people didn't flee, but I don't have records of the exact situation [as he did with rebel attacks on civilians]. There, some people are with the assailants. Those who are with the assailants, if they do not come, and the military passes through, it is at their own risk.[150]

---

[148]"Burundi army hunts down rebels in Bujumbura area," Agence France Presse, December 19, 1997.

[149]Human Rights Watch interview in Bujumbura, June 10, 1997.

[150]André Ndayizamba, governor of Bururi, Human Rights Watch interview, Bururi, June 20, 1997.

The prevailing official view is that if civilians fail to follow government orders or if they support the rebels, it is their own fault if they become military targets. Some areas where the military believes that support for the FDD is strong, such as Kanyosha and Itare in Bujumbura-Rural, Giheta and Bugendana in Gitega, and Burambi and Buyengero in Bururi, have suffered repeated military attacks on civilians and massive loss of life. A report by the U.N. Human Rights Field Operation in Burundi in October 1997 noted that FDD attacks in August and September had "triggered immediate reprisals from the army during which civilians were killed" in Bubanza, Makamba, Cibitoke, and Bujumbura-Rural.[151]

A source from Rutegama, Muramvya, explains how soldiers responded to FDD activity in his area by attacking Hutu civilians. "The assailants would come through at night. When they were tired, they would rest. When the soldiers would get word that the CNDD was there, they would call to Gitega and Bujumbura for reinforcements. When the soldiers would arrive, the rebels were already gone, so they would exact revenge against the population."[152] According to the witness, the armed forces would fire on civilians, claiming that they had supported the FDD when they passed through or that they were themselves FDD.[153] A resident of southern Bujumbura-Rural explained a similar problem with retribution in that area. "Rebels passed back and forth through the area, in the hills above, on their way between Bururi and the Kibira. Then the soldiers would come after for *nettoyage*. But there were no assailants [FDD rebels] here, or almost none, only assailants who passed through."[154]

The following are a few examples of Burundian army attacks on civilians since the July 1996 coup:

- On September 30, 1996, a large body of FDD troops passed through Rutegama, Muramvya. Fighting broke out between FDD and government troops, and a portion of the population took refuge in a local Catholic parish compound. After the fighting died down and the FDD fled, government soldiers searched the compound and surrounding area looking for straggler FDD troops. Coming

---

[151]U.N. Department of Humanitarian Affairs, IRIN, "Weekly Round-Up 25-97 of Main Events in the Great Lakes region," October 3-9, 1997.

[152]Human Rights Watch interview, June 1997.

[153]Ibid.

[154]Human Rights Watch interview in Bujumbura-Rural, June 28, 1997.

upon a group of women and children hiding in one home, soldiers opened fire, killing five immediately and wounding seven, some of whom died subsequently.[155]

• According to the Burundian human rights organization Ligue ITEKA, soldiers killed 114 people in a Pentecostal church in Kayanza on December 12, 1996. Because of fighting in the region, a number of people had sought refuge in Nyabitwe parish at Nyarurama, Butaganzwa. After spending the night in the buildings of the parish school, the soldiers entered the church building and fired on the people gathered inside. The majority of those killed were women and children.[156]

• Informants in Giheta Commune of Gitega Province report that the armed forces repeatedly attacked civilians in that commune from April to December 1996 and again in February and March 1997. Attacks in September 1996 left hundreds of bodies scattered across the hillsides of the commune. Hundreds more were killed when the armed forces began a soon aborted attempt to create two regroupment camps.[157] A group calling itself SOS Genocide printed a list in February 1997 of the names and ages of 211 people known to have been killed there by the armed forces in November and December 1996.[158] One community leader estimates that as many as 10,000 people have been killed in Giheta since April 1996 out of a population of 70,000.[159]

---

[155]Human Rights Watch interviews, June 1997.

[156]ITEKA, "Des militaires burundais massacrent 114 personnes dans une église pentecôtiste," *Bulletin d'Information de la Ligue Burundaise des Droits de l'Homme "ITEKA,"* January-March 1997.

[157]Human Rights Watch interviews in Giheta, Gitega, June 12 and June 30, 1997.

[158]S.O.S. Genocide, "Special Cadeau fin d'Année," February 1997. The document also lists fifty-six people killed in Mutaho Commune and 141 people killed in Bugendana Commune, where Human Rights Watch did not conduct investigations, as well as those killed during regroupment in Rutegama, Muramvya, mentioned in the previous chapter.

[159]Human Rights Watch interview, June 1997.

- Informants from Vugizo, Makamba, reported that civilians had been targeted in that area in April and May, 1997, because the FDD soldiers operating in the area generally left immediately after their raids. As one man told Human Rights Watch, "Soldiers can cause problems when they go into the hills and look for assailants. They loot and burn. They can accuse people of being assailants. The first attacks here were assailants, who came to burn our homes. Then the military came and burned."[160]

- The group SOS Genocide lists the name, age, and means of death of 107 people reportedly killed by the Burundian armed forces on December 13, 1996, in Ruvyagira, in Mutambu commune of Bujumbura-Rural. The majority of the victims were women and children.[161]

- Government troops fired on Hutu refugees returning from Tanzania at Giteranyi in a forced repatriation, then pursued survivors with bayonets, killing over one hundred. According to witnesses who saw the incident from the Tanzanian side, the soldiers came prepared with equipment to clean the blood from the site.[162]

- On January 11, 1997, army spokesperson Lt. Col. Isaie Nibizi admitted that the army had shot and killed 126 Hutu who had recently returned from Tanzania. According to Nibizi, the Hutu were killed when they tried to break out of a camp where they were being detained. According to Nibizi, seven soldiers were arrested in connection with this incident.[163]

- On May 14, 1997, at Kigwena, along the Lake Tanganyika coast between Rumonge and Nyanza-Lac, soldiers fired on people on the way to mass. The

---

[160]Human Rights Watch interview at Kigamba, Mabanda, June 19, 1997.

[161]S.O.S. Genocide, "Special Cadeau fin d'Année," February 1997.

[162]Human Rights Watch interview, Bujumbura, June 15, 1997.

[163]"Burundi Army Admits It Killed 126 Hutu Refugees," *New York Times*, January 12, 1997, p. 5.

attack was apparently unprovoked and left forty people dead. According to military sources, the commander of this unit has been imprisoned.[164]

- In mid-May 1997, after a landslide knocked out a bridge on the main coastal highway between Bujumbura and Bururi, the FDD established a position in the hills above Magara, a coastal town on the border between Bujumbura-Rural and Bururi. On May 14, 1997, the Burundian armed forces moved troops to Mugendo, a hill just above Magara, where they intended to establish a post from which they could attack the FDD. As the soldiers climbed the hill, they encountered a group of people holding a worship service at the Mugendo Pentecostal Church at about 3 p.m.. The soldiers opened fire, killing at least forty-two people. According to survivors and other witnesses, the attack was unprovoked and occurred while the victims were in the midst of their religious observance.[165]

- According to a variety of sources, the armed forces killed between seventy and one hundred civilians in an attack in Kabezi commune, Bujumbura-Rural, on October 20, 1997. The U.N. Department of Humanitarian Affairs quotes a member of the Burundi National Assembly's Human Rights Commission as saying, "They were looking for assailants, but they killed innocent people." The regional army commander admitted the next week that twenty-five people had been killed when his troops intervened to stop the burning of a primary school and claimed that the dead included CNDD members. Reports indicate, however, that the victims were unarmed.[166]

- On June 17, 1997, the FDD attacked the military post at Ngara in Bubanza around 10 a.m., apparently intending to take arms and other goods. A large regroupment camp is located at the post, and when the fighting began, people from the camp fled into the local Catholic parish compound or into the post

---

[164]Human Rights Watch interview in Bururi, June 20, 1997.

[165]Report by ITEKA and Human Rights Watch interviews in Bujumbura, June 26, 1997, and in Bujumbura-Rural, June 28, 1997. The Iteka report cites forty-two known dead, but other witnesses claim that the death toll may be as high as seventy-three.

[166]U.N. Department of Humanitarian Affairs, IRIN, "Emergency Update No. 276 on the Great Lakes," October 23, 1997; U.N. Department of Humanitarian Affairs, IRIN, "Emergency Update No. 279 on the Great Lakes," October 28, 1997.

itself. According to witnesses interviewed at Bubanza hospital, several soldiers were killed, and, apparently in retaliation, the military shot into the crowd of assembled Hutu, killing fifteen or more civilians. While the exact details of the attack and military response are unclear, it appear that the military killed the civilians after the FDD had fled into the hills following the raid.[167]

When massacres like those at Mugendo and Ngara occur, the military generally seeks to deflect blame either by attributing the massacres to the FDD or by claiming that the victims themselves were FDD soldiers. After the massacre at Ngara, for example, Radio Burundi, the official state radio, announced that eleven people had been killed by the FDD when they attacked the regroupment camp. Journalists and other investigators are rarely able to visit the massacre sites, and survivors are encouraged to repeat the official story. When Human Rights Watch spoke with injured survivors of the Ngara attack in Bubanza hospital, for example, there were guards near their rooms. With the guards in the hospital compounds, witnesses were reluctant to speak, and those who did claimed that they had been shot by the FDD. Vagueness and internal contradictions in their stories, however, suggested they were unable to speak freely. Other witnesses interviewed in private, well away from the military guard, told a different and much more coherent version of events, forthrightly blaming the deaths on the armed forces.[168]

Describing a particularly blatant example of attempts to deflect blame, one man from Muyinga province said that he watched from the windows of his house as a group of soldiers robbed a store. When their robbery was complete, they went into the forest and shot in the air and called out "It's the assailants [rebels]!" He said the soldiers killed people, including at least three Tutsi, and blamed it on the FDD to cover the robbery.[169]

Targeted Attacks, Summary Executions, and "Disappearances"

In addition to attacks on civilians and indiscriminate killing in combat zones, the armed forces have killed many civilians outside combat zones either in small-scale targeted attacks or through summary executions. The armed forces attacked or arrested and summarily executed either young Hutu men, who they thought could potentially join the FDD, or Hutu men and women prominent in their

---

[167]Human Rights Watch interviews in Bubanza, June 27, 1997.

[168]Human Rights Watch interviews, Bubanza hospital, June 27, 1997.

[169]Human Rights Watch interview, June 1997.

communities, such as businessmen, teachers, and politicians—in short, anyone who could potentially gain public support and organize opposition. Witnesses reported selective killings of this sort in nine of the ten provinces in which the Human Rights Watch team conducted investigations.

Human Rights Watch researchers investigated several attacks that took place during the third week of June 1997, in Nyambuye Commune, Bujumbura-Rural. On Saturday, June 14, soldiers killed six people and injured four at Gishingano, a rural community in the hills just northeast of Bujumbura. According to neighbors who witnessed the attack, the victims were gathered at a private home for a memorial service for a community member who had died. At 6:50 p.m., a small group of soldiers appeared and, apparently without provocation, shot and killed two people at the entrance to the compound. They then entered the compound and shot into the crowd gathered in the courtyard behind the house, killing four more and injuring four. When the research team visited the house three days after the incident, blood was still visible in the courtyard dirt and on the exterior walls and doorstep of the house. According to witnesses, the soldiers pillaged the home before leaving.[170]

The day after the attack, the bodies were interred in a large grave beside the house. Those killed included Pierre Claver Congera, a twenty-seven-year-old man who worked as a Catholic catechist, his twenty-five-year-old wife, and his mother. Also killed was Paul Mpawenayo, whose wife, Mpitabavuma, was killed in another incident a year earlier, according to the surviving children. Among the injured were Angeline Tatu and Caroli Nyandwi. In addition to being shot, some of the victims had their throats slashed. According to neighbors who were hiding in the area, about thirteen soldiers wearing black berets returned to the house around dawn the night of the attack along with a commandant. A man who spent the night hidden in the brush next to the compound claimed that he heard the commandant say, "Now we have begun a good work."[171]

On the same night as the attack at Gishingano, three more people were killed on a neighboring hill, Gasananzuki. According to people interviewed at the site, when the attack at Gishingano occurred, people throughout the area who heard the shots fled their homes and hid themselves in the brush. Around 8 p.m., neighbors heard cries from the manioc field where a man named Shirakandi was hiding. According to one person hiding nearby, "He cried out three times, and then it was

---

[170]Human Rights Watch interviews and investigations at Gishingano, Isare, Bujumbura-Rural, June 17, 1997.

[171]Ibid.

over." In the morning, neighbors found Shirakandi with his neck cut and his belly sliced open. The body of the younger of his two wives, Pascasie, was found where she had been hiding several hundred yards away, along with their one-and-a-half -year-old son, Willo. They had both been knifed or bayoneted to death. There were apparently no direct witnesses to the attacks, but neighbors said that they believed the attack had been carried out by soldiers, since soldiers were in the area and nothing was stolen from the victims. Human Rights Watch was shown the grave in which the bodies were buried near the field where Shirakandi had been hiding.[172]

According to area residents, military investigators came to the area following the attack, claiming that the attack had been carried out by the FDD. According to one man, "After these events, the soldiers came and took a number of people and asked them questions that they could not answer. They [the soldiers] claim that there are assailants [rebels] here, when there are none."[173]

Four days after the attacks at Gishingano and Gasananzuki, another series of attacks occurred approximately two kilometers away at Nyambuye, near a Catholic parish compound and a public school. According to numerous witnesses interviewed by Human Rights Watch, soldiers from Mparo military post arrested two young men, Celestin Ntamakuriro and Saban, the son of Simon, while on a patrol just after dusk. They bound the men, with their arms behind their backs, and took them along as they continued the patrol. Approaching the Nyambuye parish and school, the patrol passed a bar run by Ntamakuriro's family. Ntamakuriro's mother, Therese Nsakaje, his brother, Deo Mpawenimana, and his daughter, Celestine Uwimana, confronted the patrol, insisting that Ntamakuriro was from the area and was not a rebel. The soldiers responded by shooting at those who had gathered, killing the three family members, plus an elderly man who had been drinking at the bar, Michel Ntahoturi, the father of the chief of the zone. Another patron at the bar was also injured. The military patrol continued along the hill, with Ntamakuriro and Saban still in tow, until they reached a home where two young men, Mpawenibama Emmanuel and Ntahorwamiye Deo, were drinking. According to witnesses, the soldiers shot the men, saying they were CNDD. The patrol then returned back down the hill toward their camp and shot Ntamakuriro and Saban. In addition to relating these events, witnesses of the attack pointed out

---

[172]Human Rights Watch interviews and investigations at Gasanzuki, Isare, Bujumbura-Rural, June 17, 1997.

[173]Human Rights Watch interview at Gasanzuki, Isare, Bujumbura-Rural, June 17, 1997.

the research team an area along a wall across from the bar where a number of the victims were killed, as well as graves where several of the victims were buried.[174]

Certain similarities suggest that the targets for the attacks at Gishingano, Gasananzuki, and Nyambuye were not chosen simply at random. All of the victims in these attacks were Hutu. In addition, both interviews and observation indicated that those targeted for killing were among the wealthiest Hutu in their communities. Most of the victims lived in brick or cement houses, while the majority of neighboring houses were made of mud. Shirakandi was a small trader, Ntamakuriro's family ran a bar, Congera worked as a catechist, and other of the victims had off-farm employment. The victims also included a number of young men. As a number of people in various parts of the country told the Human Rights Watch research team, the selection of targets for elimination in current violence follows the pattern established in 1972 in which soldiers targeted intellectuals and other community elite.

The attacks investigated by Human Rights Watch were not isolated incidents. Area residents and others told the research team that summary executions and targeted attacks were occurring in this commune, Isare, on an almost daily basis. One person reported that soldiers killed two other young men in the area on the same day as the attacks at Gishingano and Gasananzuki. Soldiers shot Donacien Bankakaje at 2 p.m. and Adolph Ndiwanaba at 4 p.m. not far from Gishingano, both apparently without provocation.[175] One informant reported that soldiers summarily executed two of his relatives, Nicodeme, a father of five children, and Fidel, a father of four, near the location of the attack at Nyambuye.[176] Residents of Gishingano reported that soldiers killed nine people on a neighboring hill, Mwikungo, during May, while a man whose son was among those injured in the Gishingano attack said that soldiers killed another of his sons, a father of two

---

[174]Human Rights Watch investigations conducted at Nyambuye, Isare, Bujumbura-Rural, June 26, 1997. While the Human Rights Watch team was visiting the site of the first killings, a patrol of three soldiers approached and questioned the team. After the soldiers' departure, those residents who had not fled declared that the three were from Mparo military post and were among those involved in the attack. The patrol continued to the site of the second killings, where they waited for the researchers to arrive, but because residents urged the team to leave, they did so.

[175]Human Rights Watch interview in Bujumbura, June 15, 1997.

[176]Human Rights Watch interview in Bujumbura, June 26, 1997.

children, in April.[177] Sources suggest that the armed forces have regularly carried out similar attacks in several other communes of Bujumbura-Rural, including Kanyosha, Kabezi, and Muhuta, and in various other parts of the country. Interviews conducted by Refugees International researchers in November 1997 with Hutu refugees recently arrived in Tanzania from five different provinces in eastern Burundi (only one of which was a zone of combat at the time) found similar results. According to their report, the refugees "told of executions of family members, capture of villages' male residents and burning of homes and fields. ... The refugees' allegations together paint a compelling picture of a citizenry being terrorized by the army."[178]

Hutu and some moderate Tutsi political figures have been especially targeted for attack. Prior to the July 1996 coup, the military and Tutsi militias assassinated a substantial number of Hutu politicians. A document released by the opposition party Frodebu in May 1996 describes the assassination of Frodebu members including Presidents Ndadaye and Ntaryamire, thirteen governors and assistant governors, twenty-two members of parliament including four ministers, eighteen communal administrators, and a large number of other political figures between October 21, 1993 and May 15, 1996.[179] An anonymous document from April 1997 lists an additional ten members of Uprona assassinated, of which eight were Hutu assassinated by Tutsi militia.[180] On August 2, 1997, another Frodebu parliamentarian, Paul Sirahenda, was killed in Makamba. On June 30, 1997, the wife of Léonce Ngendakumana, the president of the National Assembly, was injured in a mine explosion in Bujumbura that killed her bodyguard.[181] Other politicians—including some Tutsi critics of President Buyoya—have been arrested, and in some cases tortured. A number of Hutu politicians, including some

---

[177]Human Rights Watch interviews in Gishingano, Bujumbura-Rural, June 17, 1997.

[178]Refugees International, "Findings of RI Mission to Camps in Tanzania," December 15, 1997.

[179]Parti Sahwanya Frodebu, "Génocide Cours au Burundi: Cas des Intellectuels Hutu," Bujumbura, May 15, 1996.

[180]Anonymous Document, "Liste des Representants du Peuple Suppleants du Parti Uprona qui sont dèjá morts depuis le 21 octobre 1993 jusqu'au 4 Avril 1997."

[181]U.N. Department of Humanitarian Affairs, IRIN, "Burundi: Humanitarian Situation Report, July 31-August 6, 1997," August 6, 1997.

currently serving in the Buyoya administration, told Human Rights Watch that they have serious concerns for their personal safety and the safety of their families. One Hutu government official told Human Rights Watch that he regularly has to flee his community to avoid assassination: "I have friends who protect me. When extremists want to challenge me, I am informed and I leave."[182]

In addition to targeted attacks and assassinations, the armed forces have carried out numerous summary executions throughout the country. When the FDD established a post near Mugendo in Bujumbura-Rural in late May, the military created a regroupment camp just down the coast beside their camp at Rutumo, Bururi, and they ordered all of the population of Magara and the surrounding area to assemble. A small number of people took refuge instead in the Catholic parish of Magara, including the director of the local grade schools, Yolande Cishahayo, and her two teen-aged daughters. On June 5, the commandant of the military post at Rutumo sent a letter ordering the people staying at the parish to come to the camp. The group complied, but when they arrived at the camp they were arrested, bound, and taken into the military post for questioning. All of those interrogated were released the same day except Cishahayo, who was a Tutsi married to a Hutu. According to one of Cishahayo's daughters, who was still at the military post when the questioning began, the guards asked Cishahayo, "What are you still doing here?", evidently suggesting that loyal Tutsi should not have remained in FDD-controlled territory. Around 8 p.m., people in the camp heard two gunshots, and in the morning, Cishahayo's daughter found her body along the side of the road near the camp.[183]

According to witnesses from Gitaramuka in Karuzi, the military in that commune has arrested a number of Hutu from the community who were never seen again. An informant told Human Rights Watch, "The military take people one by one on the road. On my hill they have taken people." On Monday, June 2, 1997, the military arrested a zone councillor and another man named Paul, who worked as a relief worker in a regroupment camp. The soldiers took them to the military camp at Kiyange, where they evidently questioned the two about their connection to another prisoner whom they accused of working for the FDD. On Wednesday, June 4, people living near the camp heard gunfire in the military post, and the next morning when the families of the two prisoners arrived with food for them, the soldiers told them that it was no longer necessary, implying that the men were

---

[182]Human Rights Watch interviews, June and July 1997.

[183]Human Rights Watch interviews in Bujumbura, June 26, 1997, and in Bujumbura-Rural, June 28, 1997.

dead, although they did not show the families the bodies. The same day, another man, Kameteri, was arrested after he insulted the administrator of the commune. When his wife went to look for him in the military jail, she found that he was not among the prisoners. The soldiers denied any knowledge of his whereabouts, and he has not been seen subsequently, nor has his body been discovered.[184]

At Kizuka along the Lake Tanganyika shore in Bururi Province, soldiers killed two women and four men around June 15. According to residents of the area interviewed by Human Rights Watch, the six had come down to the coast from the hills to go to the market at Kizuka. Most of the population from the hills has been regrouped around Kizuka, living with families or in temporary housing. When the six came down to the market, they were arrested by the soldiers who accused them of being rebels, although the witnesses told Human Rights Watch that the six were simply residents of the area who had come to market, not rebels. The soldiers tortured the four men in full public view, then shot and stabbed them. They took the two women to the side and raped them, then killed them. According to witnesses, one of the victims, Mineti, had three children, while another, Kabura, had four. As one witness told us, "Every day there are attacks like this. They take people coming from the market. People live in fear of the soldiers."[185]

A girl in Bihemba Regroupment camp in Karuzi reported that her nineteen-year-old brother Damien had fled to Ngozi when the military began to create regroupment camps. He returned to his community in August 1996. Just after his return a group of civilians came and arrested him, accusing him of being an FDD combattant. They turned him over to the military authorities, and he was summarily executed.[186]

When the FDD attacked Kigamba Zone in Makamba in April 1996, most of the population fled to Kayogoro, Mubera, and Vugizo. When people began to return to their homes two weeks later, they found the bodies of three men who had been summarily executed. Two of the dead were elderly and may have had difficulty fleeing. The son of one of the victims claimed that his father had been fleeing

---

[184]Human Rights Watch interviews in Karuzi, June 13, 1997.

[185]Human Rights Watch interviews at Kizuka, Bururi, July 1, 1997.

[186]Human Rights Watch interview in Bihemba Regroupment Camp, Bugenyuzi Commune, Karuzi, June 13, 1997. The young girl was unclear whether the neighbors who arrested her brother were part of a Hutu patrol or Tutsi from the Tutsi internally displaced persons (IDP) camp in the area, but from other interviews in the camp, the latter seems more probable.

when he was captured. The victims were found with their arms tied behind their backs. While no one in the community witnessed the executions, area residents told Human Rights Watch that they believed that the killings had been carried out by the armed forces.[187]

The armed forces often accuse their victims of being rebels in order to justify their attacks. According to numerous witnesses, in the regroupment camps soldiers often take young men and locally prominent Hutu and beat them, sometimes kill them, claiming that they are rebels. In addition, anyone who is unknown to the soldiers or to camp leaders is assumed to be a rebel and risks execution. The case of Léonce Nibarutu, a Hutu living in Bujumbura who was executed by soldiers when he came to Buteganzwa to visit his family, was reported in the last chapter. Another example involved a man named Mubo, a small businessman who sold tea and bread in Buteganzwa, Kayanza, prior to regroupment. He fled into the Kibira Forest in December 1996, when the military was attacking the population to force them into the regroupment camps. When Mubo returned to Buteganzwa in early June, the military immediately arrested him and beat him to death.[188]

Signs of malnutrition, such as swollen legs and bleached hair, have become a means for the military to identify people who may have been living with the rebels, since chronic malnutrition is apparently a problem in areas controlled by the CNDD such as the Kibira National Forest and the mountains along the Congo-Nile Crest in Bururi. The research team visited a health center near the Kibira forest in Kayanza where severely malnourished children and adults had come for treatment, and some of the malnourished admitted to having been with the CNDD in the forest in Cibitoke.[189] Similar cases of people leaving rebel-controlled areas because of lack of food have been reported in Bururi, Bubanza, and parts of Bujumbura-Rural.

According to Human Rights Watch investigations, however, chronic malnutrition is not restricted to rebel zones. While government officials we interviewed claimed that severe malnutrition affects only those who have been living in rebel zones—the governor of Bubanza, for example, claimed that the malnourished in local health centers had been "in the bush with the rebels"[190]—the

---

[187]Human Rights Watch interviews in Mabanda, Makamba, June 19, 1997.

[188]Human Rights Watch interview at Musema, Buteganzwa, Kayanza, July 23, 1997.

[189]Human Rights Watch Investigation in Kayanza, June 24, 1997.

[190]Human Rights Watch Interview with the Governor of Bubanza, Lt. Colonel Gerard Haziyo, on June 10, 1997.

majority of cases of chronic malnutrition we encountered were people who had been staying in government-controlled areas but had been displaced and unable to farm because of fighting or regroupment. For example, the malnourished we interviewed at Bubanza hospital had been at the regroupment camps at Ngara and Musigati for many months, and it was because they were not allowed to return home to farm while no food was provided in the camps that they faced malnutrition.[191] Health workers in Karuzi likewise insisted that the malnourished adults they were treating came from the regroupment camps, not the national park (and, hence, the rebels).[192] Even many of the severely malnourished who had come from Cibitoke to Kayanza for treatment had not been with the rebels in the forest but had been driven from their homes by persistent fighting and had been living with families or in internally displaced persons (IDP) camps, where food supplies were inadequate.[193]

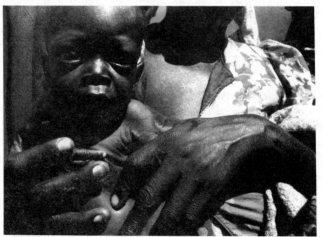

Instability means malnutrition for babies like this six-month-old in Bubanza.

---

[191]Investigations in Bubanza on June 10 and June 27, 1997.

[192]Human Rights Watch interviews in Karuzi, June 13, 1997.

[193]Human Rights Watch investigation in Kayanza, June 24, 1997.

Nevertheless, soldiers suspect anyone who suffers from malnutrition of having been with the CNDD. In the first week of June 1997 at a nutrition center near Bujumbura, soldiers dressed in civilian clothes interrogated those women waiting in the line for nutritional supplements who had white hair, a sign of severe malnutrition. According to reports given to the employees of the feeding center, soldiers waited for the women at the bottom of a hill below the feeding center, and when the women passed on their way home, they were taken and killed. The next week, all of the women who came for nutritional supplements had shaved their heads, so that the soldiers could not determine who had chronic malnutrition. It is not at all clear that these women had "been with the rebels," as the authorities claim. Many appear instead to have been living with host families because of insecurity that prevented them from returning home.[194] People in other parts of the country have been similarly targeted.

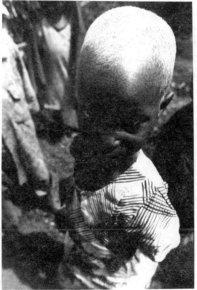

Instability has led to severe malnutrition in this girl as evidenced by her white, straight hair and eyelashes.

---

[194]Human Rights Watch interview in Bujumbura, June 10, 1997.

The Burundian government does have the right to arrest and try those individuals they suspect of personal responsibility in criminal activity. However, article 6 of Protocol II requires that prisoners arrested for criminal offenses related to the armed conflict be treated humanely and be tried in an independent and impartial court of law. Among a number of rights of the accused in penal prosecutions during armed conflict, article 6(2)(b) stipulates that "no one shall be convicted of an offence except on the basis of individual penal responsibility."[195] In the cases reported above, those killed were summarily executed. In these and other cases, the victims are not accused of specific personal criminal offenses but are considered "guilty" merely for having lived in areas controlled by the FDD or because of their prominence in the community. These extrajudicial executions, state-sanctioned murders, blatantly violate the rules of war.

Rape

Members of the Burundian Armed Forces use rape to terrorize and humiliate the civilian population. As reported above, when the military killed six people at Kizuka, Bururi, in mid-June 1997, they raped the two women in the group before killing them. According to testimonies gathered by Human Rights Watch, during attacks on civilians, members of the military frequently rape women and girls before killing them. Numerous witnesses reported that rape was widespread during the violence surrounding the creation of regroupment camps, and rape continues to be a serious problem in the camps. Health workers in Kayanza report that rape was extremely widespread during the creation of the regroupment camps and that, although rape is currently somewhat less common, women and girls who have been raped by soldiers continue to appear frequently at the health centers for treatment.[196]

Incidents of rape by the armed forces are not limited to the regroupment camps. Soldiers also rape Tutsi women who live in the camps for the internally displaced. In some cases, soldiers and other men apparently force displaced women and girls to have sex with them in exchange for food and shelter. Health workers claim that in IDP camps such as the camp near Buyenzi zone in Bujumbura, they have encountered many cases of girls as young as fourteen and fifteen who are pregnant as a result of rape and coerced sex.[197]

---

[195] Articles 6 and 7, Protocol II to the Geneva Conventions of 12 August 1949.

[196] Human Rights Watch interviews in Kayanza, June 23 and 24, 1997.

[197] Human Rights Watch interview in Bujumbura, June 10, 1997, and other interviews.

Looting and Theft

The armed forces continue to destroy civilian homes as a means of eliminating refuge for FDD combatants, forcibly displacing civilians, and preventing the organization of Hutu opposition to the regime. As reported in chapter three, the military burned thousands of houses during the process of regroupment in Karuzi, Kayanza, Bubanza, and Muramvya. The practice of looting and destroying homes spread to the south when fighting began there. Rural residents in an area of Kigamba Zone in Mabanda Commune of Makamba where many houses have been burnt told Human Rights Watch that the military had burned their homes following the FDD attack in April. In Vugizo Commune, Makamba, residents said that the military had not only burned but razed to the ground homes belonging to people who had resisted regroupment.[198] The military also burned a large number of houses in May 1997 in Rumonge, Burambi, Buyengero, and Songa communes of Bururi. The destruction of homes was evidently related to the presence of the FDD in the province and attempts to force residents to regroup.[199] The armed forces have destroyed other buildings in an effort to eliminate refuge for FDD combatants. Local people told Human Rights Watch that when the military abandoned its post in Mudende, Bururi in May, they took the roof off a public school and broke down the walls so that the building could not be used by the FDD.[200] The research team visited several homes in Isare Commune, in Bujumbura-Rural, which had recently been burned. Residents claimed that soldiers had burned their homes in May, but they did not know the motive. An attack on one of the homes, where the owner ran a small bar in the main room, seemed to fit the pattern of military attack on small businesspeople in the area.[201]

Theft, either directly by members of the armed forces or with their support or consent, is also a major problem. Wherever the armed forces have destroyed homes, they have first looted the contents, taking clothes, radios, cookware, and other portable items. Many residents of regroupment camps complained that soldiers continued to steal from them. In Karuzi, camp residents complained that even though they were now able to work their fields, soldiers commonly stole their

---

[198]Human Rights Watch interviews in Makamba, June 19, 1997.

[199]Human Rights Watch interviews in Bururi, April 21, 1997.

[200]Human Rights Watch interviews in Bururi, April 21, 1997.

[201]Human Rights Watch interviews in Nyambuye, Isare, Bujumbura-Rural, June 26, 1997.

harvests.[202]   Theft by the military is not restricted to regroupment camps. Informants reported instances of recent robberies by soldiers in Bujumbura, Bujumbura-Rural, Bururi, Karuzi, and elsewhere.

In some instances, Tutsi civilians, with support from the military, have carried out attacks against Hutu. Following the assassination of President Ndadaye in 1993, rival Hutu and Tutsi youth gangs formed in Bujumbura and elsewhere and began killing and robbing people. While some attacks by the gangs may have been politically motivated, attempting to drive members of the opposite ethnicity out of a neighborhood, others seem to have been motivated more by greed. Both Hutu and Tutsi gangs were responsible for atrocities, but witnesses claim that the Tutsi gangs—generally known as the Sans Echec ("without failure") or Sans Défaite ("without defeat")—received assistance from the military in the form of training and arms. While tolerating crime by the Tutsi youth militia, the armed forces actively sought to crush the Hutu youth militia, such as the Chicago Bulls.[203]

After the July 1996 coup, the military finally sought to bring the Tutsi gangs fully under control by incorporating most members into the armed forces (see chapter seven). Members of the armed forces have, however, continued to tolerate or actively support crime against Hutu targets. Informants in both Gitega and Bujumbura complained that Hutu suffer disproportionately from armed robberies.[204] One source in Bujumbura told Human Rights Watch that people in his neighborhood are robbed almost every night, and that those robbed are usually Hutu, "Because they do not have the connections with the military and the police that protect them." He claimed that there appeared to be complicity on the part of the police in the rampant crime in the capital.[205]

In Gitega and Karuzi, sources told Human Rights Watch that Tutsi civilians from IDP camps were involved in both killing and robbing of Hutu in those provinces. According to informants in Gitega, Tutsi from the IDP camp at Butezi, Ruyigi, have been involved in attacks on civilians in Ruyigi and Gitega. A Hutu man, Cyprien Nzigirabarya, "disappeared" on March 24, 1997, when he went to

---

[202]Human Rights Watch interviews in Karuzi, June 13, 1997.

[203]Human Rights Watch interviews in Kigali, 1996, and Bujumbura, June 17 and 25, 1997.

[204]Human Rights Watch interviews in Gitega, June 12, 1997, and Bujumbura, June 7, 1997.

[205]Human Rights Watch interview in Bujumbura, June 7, 1997.

check on property he owned in Ruyigi. According to investigations made by his wife, witnesses saw two Tutsi men from Butezi known for their involvement in Tutsi militia activity stop Nzigirabarya, apparently intending to rob him. They took him to their camp, and he was not seen again.[206]

Torture

The right not to be tortured is a core human right. Article 3 common to the four Geneva Conventions of 1949 forbids "at any time and in any place whatsoever mutilation, cruel treatment, and torture." In addition, "outrages upon personal dignity, in particular humiliating and degrading treatment" are prohibited by Common Article 3. Similarly, Article 4(2)(a) of Protocol II absolutely prohibits,

> violence to the life, health and physical or mental well-being of persons, in particular murder as well as cruel treatment such as torture, mutilation or any form of corporal punishment.

Torture is further prohibited by numerous human rights instruments, including Article 5 of the Universal Declaration of Human Rights and Article 7 of the International Covenant on Civil and Political Rights which state that "[n]o one shall be subjected to torture or to cruel, inhuman or degrading treatment or punishment."

Hutu informants commonly complained to Human Rights Watch that the armed forces of Burundi used torture and ill-treatment against the population. In Muramvya, both residents of the camps and others reported that the threat of torture or ill-treatment was a means of enforcing the requirement to participate in nightly patrols. Those who failed to participate were fined and beaten, and occasionally killed.[207] In Kayanza, Karuzi, and Muramvya, informants reported that those people who were allowed to work in their fields were beaten if they returned after the designated curfew, generally 5 or 6 p.m. Camp residents in Buteganzwa Commune of Kayanza reported that camp guards regularly beat both women and men for minor offenses.[208]

---

[206]Human Rights Watch interviews in Gitega, June 12, 1997. Human Rights Watch attempted to investigate these reports but was denied the right to conduct interviews in Butezi by the communal administrator.

[207]Human Rights Watch interviews in Rutegama Commune, Muramvya, June 11, 1997.

[208]Human Rights Watch interviews in Buteganzwa Commune, Kayanza, June 24, 1997.

Informants throughout Burundi told Human Rights Watch that as a common practice the armed forces beat people they arrest. One man in Kayanza reported that he was beaten extensively when he was arrested and held without trial for a week.[209] The Burundian human rights group Ligue ITEKA reports that Domitien Ndayizeye, the permanent executive secretary of the main opposition party Frodebu, was tortured after being arrested on February 22, 1997.[210] According to another source, the soldiers who tortured Ndayizeye were trying to force him to disclose the password to a Frodebu computer they had confiscated.[211]

Violations of the Right to Freedom of Movement

In contrast to regroupment, which forces people into camps against their will, in some areas of the country people who have fled their homes have chosen to seek safety in camps for the internally displaced. Although most of the internally displaced have been Tutsi, some Hutu have also sought to gather in places of refuge, some fleeing zones of persistent combat such as Cibitoke and others driven from their homes as a result of attacks by ethnic militia and fighting between rival youth gangs. During its travels through Burundi, the Human Rights Watch research team encountered a few areas where Hutu and Tutsi continued to live together in relative harmony—primarily in Gitega, Makamba, and Bururi—but these multi-ethnic areas were exceptional. As a result of militia and gang violence, most of Burundi has been segregated along ethnic lines since late 1995. Hutu attacks on Tutsi in the countryside drove most Tutsi either to the cities or into camps for the internally displaced, where they could be protected by soldiers. Attacks by Tutsi militia, such as the Sans Echec and Sans Défaite, drove most Hutu out of the cities. Most fled to the countryside or into refugee camps in Tanzania or Zaire, but some Hutu from Bujumbura and the surrounding area formed camps, mostly at church sites where they believed they would be protected by their numbers and by the authority of the church. Hutu in certain other areas, such as Cibitoke and Bubanza, have gathered in camps after fleeing fighting in their home communities.

---

[209]Human Rights Watch interviews in Buteganzwa Commune, Kayanza, June 24, 1997.

[210]ITEKA, "Le secrétaire exécutif permanent du FRODEBU arrêté, torturé, et relaché, *Bulletin D'Information de la Ligue Burundaise des Droits de l'Homme "ITEKA,"* January-March 1997.

[211]Human Rights Watch interview, Bujumbura, June 25, 1997.

Since taking power, the Buyoya regime has attempted to close a number of camps for internally displaced Hutu in Bujumbura and elsewhere. In March 1997, the military entered two sites for displaced Hutu in Kamenge and forced out anyone who was not from Bujumbura province, claiming that people had to live within their home province. From one camp, the military forced out 4,000 people and about 3,000 from the other, mostly people from the nearby hillsides of Bujumbura-Rural.[212] People in the camps told Human Rights Watch that they had fled into the camps because soldiers or Tutsi militia had attacked their neighborhoods and destroyed their homes, and they expressed fear that they would be killed if they went home.[213] Driving through neighborhoods which were formerly predominantly Hutu, such as Kamenge, the destruction is quite evident.

On September 11, 1997, the army announced plans to close the two Kamenge IDP camps entirely. The military claimed the closure was necessary for security reasons, because the camps harbored criminals involved in murders and armed robberies. However, according to the human rights NGO Ligue ITEKA, the sixteen attacks that occurred in the area between April and July, 1997, were attributed to members of the armed forces.[214] Human Rights Watch investigations in the region confirm that a number of the robberies and killings in the area were carried out by soldiers.

The weekend of October 18-19, 1997, the armed forces carried out a campaign to remove unauthorized people from Gatumba, a suburb 15 kilometers from Bujumbura whose population had swollen from 6,000 before 1993 to more than 100,000, including refugees from the Democratic Republic of Congo and Burundian Hutu from Bujumbura, Cibitoke, and other places where they have faced violence. In the weekend sweep of the area, police arrested more than 10,000 people without proper residence permits. Although most of these were subsequently released, many after paying fines, several thousands remained in police custody.[215]

---

[212]Human Rights Watch interviews in Bujumbura, June 8 and June 16, 1997.

[213]Human Rights Watch interviews in Bujumbura, June 16, 1997.

[214]"Burundi shuts down two 'displaced people' camps near capital," Agence France Presse, September 11, 1997.

[215]"Police Arrest Thousands in Burundi Identity Checks," Agence France Presse, October 21, 1997; "Burundi: Thousands Said Detained for Identity Checks," Radio-Television Nationale du Burundi, October 22, 1997.

The problem of denying refuge and forcing return is not restricted to Bujumbura. Some Hutu in Makamba also told Human Rights Watch that they had been forced out of IDP camps where they had gone voluntarily when FDD attacks in the area began. Tutsi were allowed to remain in the camps.[216]

Human Rights Watch visited a camp formed in June 1997 in Rwegura, Kayanza, by people fleeing fighting in Cibitoke and the Kibira Forest. Many of the people who came to this site, which formed on a hillside below a health center, were severely malnourished and had come to the site seeking medical treatment and nutritional supplements. In November 1997, the armed forces closed the site, forcing the 5,300 residents back to Cibitoke. The army spokesperson claimed that the residents of the camp had left "on their own accord because they know that they will be better off at home than in the camp." However, Doctors Without Borders reported that "the population of the camp was sent to Cibitoke, accompanied by soldiers, and then the camp was entirely burned down."[217] A number of camp residents told Human Rights Watch that they were afraid to return home because of the continuing threat of violence from the armed forces of Burundi or the insurgent groups. Several said that they had been ordered out of their homes by armed forces official.[218] Responding to criticism from Doctors Without Borders, the U.N. Humanitarian Coordinator for Burundi, Hussein Khan, and others, the army spokesman tried to link the expulsions to the closure of regroupment camps. "When people are grouped together for their security, nongovernmental organizations scream human rights violations. ... When they go home, it's the same thing. What do they want?"[219]

In November 1997, the armed forces of Burundi and Rwanda, with the backing of Congolese authorities, launched a campaign to expel Hutu from around Uvira and Bukavu in the Democratic Republic of Congo. According to the U.N. Department of Humanitarian Affairs, more than 2,000 people were driven into Burundi, including at least 125 Congolese citizens who were caught in the sweep.

---

[216]Human Rights Watch interviews in Makamba, June 19, 1997.

[217]"Army expels 5,000 displaced people from Burundi camp: MSF," Agence France Presse, November 7, 1997; U.N. Department of Humanitarian Affairs, IRIN, "Emergency Update No. 288 on the Great Lakes," November 8-10, 1997; U.N. Department of Humanitarian Affairs, IRIN, "Weekly Round-up 31-97," November 14-20, 1997.

[218]Human Rights Watch interviews in Kayanza, June 24, 1997.

[219]"Army Expels 5,000," Agence France Presse.

Aid workers have reported that the government claims those forced to return are "infiltrators, thieves, who have been stealing cattle," but those forcibly repatriated include small children.[220]

Like regroupment, forcing people who seek refuge to return to their homes against their will is a violation of the right to freedom of movement and the right to choose one's residence guaranteed in Article 12 of the International Covenant on Civil and Political Rights. The forced return practiced by the Burundian armed forces cannot be justified as necessary for protecting national security nor public order. The motivation has instead been asserting control over the Hutu population and cannot be justified under ICCPR obligations.

Furthermore, the forced return of Hutu civilians has clearly placed them in physical danger. A number of residents of Bujumbura-Rural told Human Rights Watch that they had been forced out of the camps in Kamenge. After being forced home, they were given no assistance to rebuild their houses. Since people have returned to their hills, soldiers have regularly harassed them, attacking homes, arresting people, and carrying out summary executions. (Several cases are described above.) A number of people said that they would return to the camps in Kamenge if they were allowed, because they did not feel safe in their communities. At the time Human Rights Watch visited the area in June 1997, people were spending the night outside in the bush out of fear that soldiers would kill them in their homes.[221] In Makamba, Hutu residents expressed a desire to remain at IDP camps to be protected from FDD attacks which were occurring nightly in the area, but they were sent home in June by the military while Tutsi remained in the camps. People in Makamba were also spending their nights outside for fear of attacks.[222]

---

[220]U.N. Department of Humanitarian Affairs, IRIN, "Update No. 293 for Central and Eastern Africa," November 15-17, 1997; U.N. Department of Humanitarian Affairs, IRIN, "Update No. 316 For Central and Eastern Africa," December 18, 1997.

[221]Human Rights Watch interviews in Bujumbura-Rural, June 17 and 26, 1997.

[222]Human Rights Watch interviews in Makamba, June 19, 1997.

Forced Labor

According to Article 8 of the International Covenant on Civil and Political Rights, "No one shall be required to perform forced or compulsory labour."[223] The International Labor Organization Convention on the Abolition of Forced Labor of 1959 specifically prohibits forced labor "as a means of political coercion or education" and "as a means of racial, social, national or religious discrimination."[224]

In Burundi, since the July 1996 coup, the armed forces have required Hutu civilians to provide labor without compensation in clear violation of these obligations. Forced labor is most widespread in the regroupment camps, where the armed forces have extensive control over the population. Informants in Karuzi reported that, among other tasks, they were required to carry water for the soldiers at the camp and to provide charcoal. One informant at Bugenyuzi Camp in Karuzi told Human Rights Watch, "We have no problems with the soldiers as long as we work for them." According to this and other informants, if residents of the camp do not work for the soldiers they are beaten or face other penalties.[225]

Forced labor is not restricted to the regroupment camps. Informants in Gitega reported that the armed forces have required residents of that province to provide charcoal for the troops without payment. The production of charcoal is an extremely time-consuming process, which involves searching for green wood, chopping and preparing the wood, building and monitoring the fires to produce the charcoal, and then packaging the finished product for transportation. Under ordinary circumstances, families would produce charcoal only a few times a year. However, as the size of the armed forces has expanded, the military has required each hill to provide charcoal once or twice a week.[226] The forced labor for charcoal production is required exclusively of Hutu citizens and thus violates obligations forbidding the discriminatory application of forced labor.

---

[223] Article 8, 1a, International Covenant on Civil and Political Rights, United Nations General Assembly resolution 2200 A (XXI), December 16, 1966. Entered into force on March 23, 1976.

[224] Article I, Abolition of Forced Labor Convention, International Labor Organization No. 105, 320 UNTS 291, entered into force January 17, 1959.

[225] Human Rights Watch interview in Bugenyuzi, Karuzi, June 13, 1997.

[226] Human Rights Watch interviews in Gitega, June 30, 1997.

V. HUMAN RIGHTS ABUSES BY THE ARMED FORCES FOR THE DEFENSE OF DEMOCRACY (FDD) AND OTHER REBEL GROUPS

Since taking up arms against the government of Burundi in 1993, the Forces for the Defense of Democracy (FDD), the armed wing of the National Council for the Defense of Democracy, has become the main armed opposition to the government of Burundi and, since the July 1996 coup, the Buyoya regime, displacing the formerly pre-eminent Party for the Liberation of the Hutu People (Parti pour la Liberation du Peuple Hutu, Palipehutu), which continues to operate in Cibitoke and Bubanza. Originally based in Zaire, the ADFL victory in late 1996 forced the FDD to move most of its operations to Tanzania. A third group, the Front for National Liberation (Front pour la Libération Nationale, Frolina), also based in Tanzania, ended an eighteen-month self-imposed cease fire after the armed forces of Burundi launched raids into Tanzania. Several smaller groups are also waging armed opposition to the government, including a recent splinter from the FDD, named Benjamin after its leader, which launched attacks in Cibitoke in November 1997. The FDD, Palipehutu, and other groups have engaged in numerous abuses of human rights. The rebel groups have indiscriminately attacked civilians, killing and raping, and they have assassinated unarmed political officials. They have also engaged extensively in looting and destruction of property, exacerbating serious problems of malnutrition in the country. Within areas that they control, the FDD and Palipehutu have coerced civilians to remain in the areas against their will, forcing them to farm for them and provide other labor.

Indiscriminate Attacks on Civilians

A number of sources told Human Rights Watch that the FDD "does not kill civilians." As one expatriate asserted, the commonly held belief was that, "They pillage, but they do not kill."[227] While it is true that the Burundian armed forces have been responsible for the majority of civilian deaths during the civil war, Human Rights Watch has documented a number of cases in which the FDD attacked and killed civilians. The FDD has killed civilians both in indiscriminate attacks and in targeted assassinations.

During a major offensive that began in April in the southern provinces of Makamba and Bururi, the FDD deliberately killed civilians in several locations. On April 17, 1997, the FDD attacked the commune of Mabanda in Makamba and killed a large number of civilians in Kayogoro Zone. A large group of civilians

---

[227]Human Rights Watch interview, Bujumbura, June 1997.

was killed at Murara Pentecostal Church. Human Rights Watch interviewed three survivors of the attack, one Hutu and two Tutsi. According to one of the survivors,

> The attack occurred at the end of April. We saw assailants coming down this hill [where the interview was being conducted]. It was around 10 a.m. We ran when we saw them coming. Some others stayed. The assailants assembled people in the buildings at Murara parish. They made the people enter the buildings. Some people fled. The assailants demanded money. They pointed guns at the crowd and demanded money. The refugees [the people gathered in the church] were both ethnicities. There were about twenty rebels, including one woman. Some carried machetes, and there were only four who had guns.[228]

All three witnesses lost members of their immediately families in the attack. One man lost two sons, ages thirteen and twelve. Another lost his mother and two brothers, ages twenty and eighteen. The third lost his five-year-old son.[229] The administrator of Mabanda Commune told Human Rights Watch that, including the victims at the church, the FDD killed more than one hundred people at Kayagoro. Both the administrator and the survivors asserted that the majority of those killed were Hutu. The administrator told Human Rights Watch that a rivalry between religious groups may have been a reason for the killings, since those killed were primarily Pentecostals, while most of the area youth who have joined the FDD have come from the Church of Unity in the Holy Spirit in Burundi (EUSEBU), a local sect.[230]

An attack two weeks later on the Junior Seminary at Buta received extensive media coverage because most of those killed were children. According to a report by the Catholic Bishop of Bururi,

> The morning of April 30 around 5:30, an armed group attacked the Junior Seminary of Buta. All the homes were attacked at the same time. The

---

[228]Human Rights Watch interview in Kayogoro Zone, Mabanda Commune, Makamba, June 19, 1997.

[229]Human Rights Watch interviews in Kayogoro Zone, Mabanda Commune, Makamba, June 19, 1997.

[230]Human Rights Watch interview with Déo Sindayihebura Mabanda, Makamba, June 18, 1997.

dormitories of the students, the homes of the teachers, the convent of priests, the Center of Permanent Training were fired upon simultaneously. The gunfire caused the death of forty students, wounded twenty-six seriously, two of whom are still recovering from their wounds; the burning of a dormitory, the destruction of five vehicles, the demolition of equipment, doors and windows.[231]

According to the governor of Bururi, the bishop, and other sources, the FDD combatants gathered students and a few teachers from the Junior Seminary in one hall and attempted to separate the Tutsi from the Hutu, but the Hutu refused to be separated. The combatants then sprayed the room with bullets, killing thirty-four students, who ranged in age from eleven to twenty, and six teachers.[232] Supporters of the FDD do not deny that their troops attacked the school but claim that the FDD fired upon the students only because they were first fired upon by students and/or teachers from school buildings.[233]

On the same day as the massacre at Buta, the FDD attacked the nearby village of Kiremba, just outside Bururi town. One of the first people to arrive on the scene at Kiremba following the attack told Human Rights Watch,

I was the first to arrive, with a military escort. They [the FDD] had burned the health center. We found two younger women and one old woman dead. The two younger women had been raped. They were lying with their clothes torn and their legs spread out, so I went to find some cloth to cover them up. They had been stabbed and shot. Among those killed, there were only two Tutsi, and the rest were Hutu. These were Hutu who refused to go along with the rebels.[234]

---

[231]Bernard Bududira, Bishop of Bururi, "Le massacre des petits seminaristes de Buta est 'un crime contre l'innocence et contre l'avenir' denonciation du directeur de l'UNESCO Federico Mayor," May 7, 1997. Translated from French by Human Rights Watch.

[232]"Massacres Reported at Catholic Seminary," *All Africa Press Service*, May 6, 1997.

[233]Les Chrétiens Catholiques de Bujumbura, Burundi, "L'Eveque de Bururi: Un Prélat Egaré ou un Simple Pasteur Perdu?," Bujumbura, May 19, 1997. Human Rights Watch did not interview any eyewitnesses of the attack at Buta.

[234]Human Rights Watch interview in Bururi, July 1, 1997.

According to the witness, the FDD killed a total of fourteen people in the attack at Kiremba. The FDD killed other civilians in Songa, Rutovu, and Bururi communes on the same day.[235]

The FDD has also killed civilians in Nyanza-Lac in Makamba, the southernmost commune in Burundi, which has experienced the most sustained fighting since the April FDD offensive. Several Tutsi women from Nyanza-Lac who had taken refuge in Mabanda commune told Human Rights Watch that rebels had killed a number of their family members in Nyanza Lac. One elderly woman said, "I am the only one left."[236] Burundian military sources reported on July 17, 1997 that the FDD killed fifty-one civilians, including thirty-six children and twelve women, in an attack on a village in Nyanza-Lac in July. The bodies were found in a mass grave in an area where forty-eight houses were burned.[237] The Burundian New Agency reported that rebels killed at least one civilian during an attack on Rumonge town, Bururi, on August 7.[238] Neither report was independently confirmed.

The FDD has killed civilians in other military operations as well. According to ITEKA, on February 17, 1997, at around 11 p.m., a group of rebels attacked the Pentecostal center of Mugara, near Rumonge. The combatants attacked the home of the church's pastor, killing his wife and beating his children, one of whom died as a result of his injuries. The rebels took the head of the Biblical center, whom they called by name, and killed him after a short interrogation. They pillaged the parish workshop, the home of a Swedish missionary, and other buildings, and killed a total of thirteen, six of whom were children.[239] According to U.N. reports,

---

[235]Human Rights Watch interviews in Bururi, June 20-21 and July 1, 1997.

[236]Human Rights Watch interviews, Mabanda, Makamba, June 18, 1997.

[237]"Burundi—51 Die, Others Missing After Rebel Attack in South," Agence France Presse, July 18, 1997; "More than 70 reported killed in Burundi," Reuters, July 17, 1997.

[238]"Burundi—One Killed in Rebel Attack on Rumonge Town," Agence Burundi Presse, August 7, 1997.

[239]ITEKA, "Attaque d'un Centre pentecôtiste par des "assaillants" à Mugara: 13 morts dont 6 enfants," *Bulletin d'Information de la Ligue Burundaise des Droits de l'Homme "ITEKA"*, January-March 1997, pp. 12-13.

the FDD killed fifteen people in an attack on the town of Gatete, along the Lake Tanganyika road south of Rumonge on January 17, 1997.[240]

Hutu sources from Cibitoke who had come to a site at Rwegura, Kayanza, seeking medical treatment, primarily for illnesses related to malnutrition, told Human Rights Watch that rebels regularly attack civilians who live under government control rather than in areas under their control. One woman said, "Some people from Ndora are with the military. The assailants fire on these people. They come at night and they fire on the peasants and kill people. They killed my brother-in-law. They do a sorting of the population. They search for those with money and beer."[241] Other informants from Cibitoke reported cases of civilians killed by the rebels. One man from Buhayira zone in Murwi Commune of Cibitoke told Human Rights Watch that on his hill of Mutumbu the rebels had killed Karenzo, Bucuni, and Mbigira in 1996 and Minani and Nyabenda in May 1997.[242] In Rugombo commune, Cibitoke, twenty-two people were killed by machetes in an attack attributed to the FDD on January 13, 1997. According to government sources, the community was attacked because of its failure to support the CNDD.[243]

The U.N. Human Rights Field Operation in Burundi reported a sharp increase in rebel attacks on civilians in September and October 1997 in Cibitoke, Bubanza, Bujumbura-Rural, Bururi, and Makamba. At least twenty-five people were killed and thirty-nine injured in attacks at Mabayi, Cibitoke, and Karenzi, Bubanza, on October 12, 1997.[244] Government and military officials reported a number of attacks by Hutu insurgents on civilians in November 1997 as well. According to an army report, an attack by insurgents killed thirteen in Magara, Bujumbura-Rural, on November 1, 1997. An attack in Kinyama, Cibitoke, on November 13, 1997,

---

[240]United Nations Department of Humanitarian Affairs, "U.N. Humanitarian Situation Report—Burundi (01/14-28)," January 31, 1997.

[241]Human Rights Watch interview in Muruta Commune, Kayanza, June 24, 1997.

[242]Human Rights Watch interviews in Muruta Commune, Kayanza, June 24, 1997.

[243]United Nations Department of Humanitarian Affairs, "U.N. Humanitarian Situation Report—Burundi (01/14-28)," January 31, 1997.

[244]U.N. Department of Humanitarian Affairs, IRIN, "Weekly Roundup 25-97 of Main Events in the Great Lakes Region," October 3-9, 1997; U.N. Department of Humanitarian Affairs, IRIN, "Emergency Update No. 288 on the Great Lakes," November 8-10, 1997.

killed nine, an attack at Mutimbizi, Bujumbura-Rural, on November 15, 1997, left eight dead and six wounded, and an attack on the tea factory at Buhoro, Cibitoke, on November 16, 1997, killed fourteen.[245] Agence France Presse reported a survivor of the attack at Mutimbizi as saying, "They mainly wanted to kill, but they also demanded money. We told them we had nothing, that we were poor. They stole the few pitiful things we had—women's clothing, my bicycle—and then they started killing."[246] Sources attributed several of the attacks in Cibitoke to a newly formed insurgent group called Benjamin, named after its leader, who was formerly a member of the FDD. Sources attributed other attacks to Palipehutu or the FDD. According to the army spokesman, Palipehutu hilled thirty-two civilians in an attack in Cibitoke on January 19, 1998.[247]

Since the July 1996 coup, the FDD has targeted vehicles, especially those transporting goods into Bujumbura and other cities, apparently in an attempt to disrupt economic activity and compound the effects of the international embargo. Civilians have been killed in a number of these attacks. On January 17, 1997, three people were killed in an ambush on the road between Bujumbura and Rumonge.[248] Two children were killed in an attack on a minibus traveling between Bururi town and Rumonge on June 21, 1997. The assailants shot and robbed the passengers, injuring seven others.[249]

In a series of attacks that began in June 1997, rebel groups have attacked predominantly Hutu regroupment camps or other camps for internally displaced people. The Mitakataka Camp was created in late May 1997 by Hutu from Rumata and Zina in Bubanza, mostly refugees repatriated from Zaire who had been living in other camps in Bubanza since early 1997. According to camp residents, on the

---

[245]U.N. Department of Humanitarian Affairs, IRIN, "Emergency Update No, 283 on the Great Lakes," November 1-3, 1997; U.N. Department of Humanitarian Affairs, IRIN, "Emergency Update No. 295 for Central and Eastern Africa," November 19, 1997; "Armed Rebels in Burundi Kill 22," Agence France Presse, November 18, 1997.

[246]"Armed Rebels in Burundi Kill 22," Agence France Presse.

[247]U.N. Department of Humanitarian Affairs, IRIN, "Emergency Update No. 338 for Central and Eastern Africa," January 22, 1998.

[248]United Nations Department of Humanitarian Affairs, "U.N. Humanitarian Situation Report—Burundi (01/14-28)," January 31, 1997.

[249]Human Rights Watch interview in Bujumbura, June 25, 1997.

night of June 6-7, a group of FDD troops attacked the camp. One witness recounts, "I was sleeping. I woke up and went outside and saw a house burning. We tried to save the furniture and things inside. Then I saw them [the attackers] with flames. I took my bicycle and fled. There were many men with guns. The assailants [FDD] fired in the direction of the soldiers [a military post approximately 1 kilometer to the south] to keep them from coming."[250] The FDD apparently attacked the camp intending to drive residents out. They burned houses to the ground, but did not loot from the residents. According to witnesses, people spent the night in the bush. The next day, some people fled to neighboring camps, while others remained at Mitakataka. A group of FDD combatants returned to the camp at approximately 3 p.m. and fired, killing one soldier and one civilian.[251]

The motivation for the attack at Mitakataka remains unclear. A soldier guarding the site after the attack claimed that the camp had blocked a path that the FDD used to transport supplies. Some aid workers believed that the attack might have been intended to oppose regroupment and force Hutu back to their homes.[252]

The FDD attacked another regroupment camp at Ngara, Bubanza, on June 17, 1997. This camp, like many others, was built around a military post. According to witnesses, the FDD attacked the post to pillage arms, food, and other items and did not directly target civilians. Following their armed attack, the armed forces killed at least fifteen persons in the camp.[253]

According to U.N. reports, rebel groups attacked regroupment camps in Kayanza and Bubanza in September, 1997. In one attack in Rango commune, Kayanza, in late September, rebels burned 900 shelters. According to military officials, fourteen people were killed in a November 7, 1997, attack on the regroupment camp at Rutumo, on the border between the provinces of Bururi and Bujumbura-Rural.[254]

---

[250]Human Rights Watch interview in Bubanza, June 10, 1997.

[251]Human Rights Watch interviews in Bubanza, June 10 and 27, 1997.

[252]Human Rights Watch interviews in Bujumbura and Bubanza, June 1997.

[253]Human Rights Watch interviews in Bubanza, June 27, 1997.

[254]U.N. Department of Humanitarian Affairs, IRIN, "Emergency Update No. 263 on the Great Lakes," October 4-6, 1997; U.N. Department of Humanitarian Affairs, IRIN, "Emergency Update No. 287 on the Great Lakes, November 7, 1997.

According to witnesses at the multi-ethnic IDP camp located at Gishiha Pentecostal church in Vugizo commune of Makamba, the FDD launched a major attack on the camp on April 18. FDD combatants attacked the camp, which houses approximately 6,000 people in a complex of buildings that includes a secondary school, from several sides, but the soldiers stationed at the camp fought off the attackers and there were no civilian casualties.[255]

During the months of July, August, and September, an estimated 600 civilians were killed in fighting in Cibitoke and Bubanza between the FDD and rival group Palipehutu. After its foundation in a Hutu refugee camp in Tanzania in 1980, Palipehutu became the main Hutu opposition movement in exile. During the late 1980s and early 1990s, Palipehutu was involved in incursions into northern Burundi and several attacks on the armed forces.[256] According to reports collected by the United Nations Department of Humanitarian Affairs, the two groups began fighting in July 1997 over the CNDD's plans to participate in negotiations with the Buyoya government and rivalry arising from Palipehutu's loss of support to the CNDD. The fighting killed an estimated 600 civilians living in areas of Bubanza and Cibitoke controlled by the rebel groups and drove another 30,000 civilians out of the hills and into government-controlled territory in Bubanza and several thousand more into Kayanza.[257]

Rape

In some of their attacks, the FDD and other rebel groups have engaged in rape of women and girls. An informant who witnessed the aftermath of the FDD attack at Kiremba, Bururi, on April 30, 1997, reported that at least two of the victims were raped before being killed. He told Human Rights Watch he found the women lying on their backs with their clothes ripped off and their legs spread.[258]

---

[255]Human Rights Watch interviews in Gishiha, Vugizo, Makamba, June 19, 1997.

[256]René Lemarchand, *Burundi: Ethnocide as Discourse and Practice* (Cambridge: Cambridge University Press, 1994).

[257]U. N. Department of Humanitarian Affairs, IRIN, "Emergency Update No. 228 for the Great Lakes," August 13, 1997; U.N. Department of Humanitarian Affairs, IRIN, "Emergency Update No. 252 on the Great Lakes," September 19, 1997.

[258]Human Rights Watch interview in Bururi, July 1, 1997.

Assassinations and Other Targeted Attacks on Civilians

In addition to killing civilians in indiscriminate attacks, the FDD and its supporters have assassinated a number of civilians whom they consider collaborators with the Buyoya regime. For example, on June 7, 1997, a man was stabbed to death in the camp for the internally displaced at the Johnson Center in Kamenge sector of Bujumbura. According to neighbors, attackers came out of the hills above Kamenge, an area where the FDD is believed to be active, and stabbed the man, then fled. The man was widely rumored to be a military informer and was often seen in the company of soldiers. He was not armed.[259]

Politicians, both Hutu and Tutsi, have been a major target of FDD assassination. In nearly every province where Human Rights Watch conducted interviews, people reported that the FDD had killed local politicians. For example, in Karuzi informants said that the FDD had killed the chief of Bonero Sector and Kazinga, a counselor from Buhinge, sometime after the formation of the regroupment camps.[260] The FDD killed the head of Magara Zone in Bujumbura-Rural on February 17, 1997.[261] On June 3, 1997, FDD combatants captured the chief of Mubondo-Kiganda sector in Mabanda commune of Makamba. They stole his livestock and household goods, and he is presumed dead.[262] The FDD reportedly tortured and killed the chief of Rutsiba zone as a collaborator.[263]

Since Hutu constitute 85 percent of the population—and an even higher percentage in rural areas—the FDD might be expected to avoid alienating those that it views as its primary constituency. Hence, the numbers of killings of Hutu is relatively small. A number of Tutsi civilians, however, told Human Rights Watch that they believe that the FDD targets Tutsi as a group for attack, and several cases of FDD attacks on Tutsi civilians suggest that there is validity to these fears. A larger scale killing of Tutsi took place on May 28, 1996, when FDD combatants attacked a camp for internally displaced Tutsi at Butezi, Ruyigi. Forty-nine people

---

[259]Human Rights Watch interviews in Bujumbura, June 8, 1997.

[260]Human Rights Watch interviews in Karuzi, June 13, 1997.

[261]Human Rights Watch interview in Bujumbura-Rural, June 28, 1997.

[262]Human Rights Watch interview in Mabanda, Makamba, June 18, 1997.

[263]Human Rights Watch interviews, Bujumbura, June 15, 1997.

were killed in the attack.[264]   According to informants in Buyengero, FDD combatants attacked a Tutsi family there in November 1996. The family was defended by its Hutu neighbors, who were injured in the attack. Human Rights Watch spoke with two children of the Hutu family who were injured in the attack and saw the scars from machete wounds. The FDD also burned Tutsi homes in Buyengero, Burambi, and Rumonge.[265]   A medical worker said that a group of forty-two Tutsi women and children had been treated in a Bujumbura hospital after an FDD attack in Cibitoke in May 1997. All of the victims suffered from machete wounds to the head.[266]

The fact that more Tutsi civilians have not been killed by the rebel groups and their supporters since the July 1996 coup may be due to the protection that the armed forces provide to Tutsi. After the assassination of Ndadaye, Hutu militia killed thousands of Tutsi civilians throughout the country, and Tutsi in rural areas of provinces such as Muramvya, Gitega, Ngozi, and Karuzi took refuge in camps where they received protection from the military. Some 300,000 people, the vast majority of them Tutsi, remain in camps for the internally displaced, most of which are closely guarded by government troops. A group of Tutsi women who lived in a camp in Muramvya told Human Rights Watch that they feel the soldiers protect them from the rebels. "Prior to the camps there was disorder. We couldn't go into our fields. Many people lost their lives when they went into their fields."[267] A Hutu source in Muramvya explained that Hutu feel uncomfortable because the Tutsi remain in camps under military protection. "As long as the two ethnicities are separated, the Hutu feel vulnerable."[268]

---

[264]Human Rights Watch, *Human Rights Watch World Report 1997*, (New York: Human Rights Watch, December 1996), p. 20. The Human Rights Watch research team visited the Butezi IDP camp in June 1997 but was prevented by local authorities from conducting interviews with camp residents.

[265]Human Rights Watch interviews in Buyengero, Bururi, June 21, 1997.

[266]Human Rights Watch interview in Bujumbura, June 7, 1997.

[267]Human Rights Watch interviews in Rutegama, Muramvya, June 11, 1997.

[268]Human Rights Watch interview in Rutegama, Muramvya, June 11, 1997.

Looting, Theft, and Destruction of Property

The FDD and other insurgent groups have engaged extensively in looting and theft. In all the regions of rebel activity where Human Rights Watch conducted research, the population—both Hutu and Tutsi—complained that the FDD raided their homes and stole cattle, clothes, household items, and money. In some areas, people complained that the FDD have coerced them into providing food, money, and other support. Pillaging is by far the greatest complaint Hutu make against the FDD.

Since the beginning of their major offensive in April 1997 in Bururi and Makamba, the FDD has engaged in massive looting of the civilian population. The general impression among the Hutu civilians in much of Bururi and Makamba is that pillaging is the main offense of the FDD. As one religious worker told Human Rights Watch regarding the FDD attacks in Bururi in April, "The assailants killed very few victims. They pillaged and burned, but they did not kill. ... The rebels generally burn or loot, but there are no victims, or very few."[269]

FDD combatants have repeatedly raided civilian households in Mabanda and Vugizo communes of Makamba. One man from Kigamba zone of Mabanda told Human Rights Watch that the FDD had attacked his home in late May. They stole three cows, seven goats, and clothing, and they burned his kitchen.[270] According to residents of Mabanda and Vugizo, the FDD was conducting looting raids on a nightly basis. On June 14, 1997, the rebels attacked Gahundu in Vugizo and took a large number of cattle. A local resident said, "We know it was the rebels, because they took the cattle in the direction of Nyanza-Lac [the main FDD base in the area]." Because of these attacks, residents claimed that no one sleeps in their house at night. "We do not want to be killed at home."[271] Residents of Kayogoro zone of Mabanda reported that from their hiding places in the bush they could see the rebels coming down from the hills in the direction of Nyanza-Lac to raid their houses at night, because they carried flashlights.[272]

Human Rights Watch spoke with three women along the Lake Tanganyika shore in Bururi several hours after FDD assailants robbed them at gunpoint. According to the women, who had been regrouped and lived with families in

---

[269]Human Rights Watch interview in Bururi, June 20, 1997.

[270]Human Rights Watch interview in Kigamba zone, Mabanda, Makamba, June 19, 1997.

[271]Human Rights Watch interviews in Mabanda, Makamba, June 19, 1997.

[272]Human Rights Watch interviews in Kayogoro, Mabanda, Makamba, June 19, 1997.

Rumonge, they had left Rumonge town to go into their fields around 7 a.m. On the way, they were stopped by several armed men in civilian clothes. They took all of the money that the women had with them. Several other people were attacked in the area the same morning. Soldiers pursued the attackers, but they escaped into the hills above Rumonge.[273]

Several women who were in Bubanza Hospital told Human Rights Watch that they were injured when the FDD attacked Musigati Regroupment Camp on June 20. According to the women, the main goal of the attack was to loot from camp residents. "They came and pillaged. They took money, clothes, animals, pots and pans and other things from the kitchen."[274] Several people were shot during the attack, although it was unclear whether they were shot by the FDD or by government troops.

Article 4(2)(g) of Protocol II prohibits pillaging. By taking food and other items essential to the survival of the civilian population, the rebel groups in Burundi have violated these prohibitions and contributed to the deterioration of the humanitarian situation. Informants at Kizina Regroupment Camp in Bubanza told Human Rights Watch that pillaging by the FDD contributed to hunger in the area. "Even now when we plant, the harvest is pillaged by the assailants. The assailants pass through and pillage at night. People see them passing, because everyone sleeps in the fields. We are afraid to sleep in our homes."[275]

At Minago, along the Lake Tanganyika shore in Bururi, approximately 6,000 people are regrouped. They spend the days in houses in the town and the nights in the local health center and Catholic parish compound, an arrangement that allows for better sanitation than in many regroupment sites. However, the FDD has repeatedly cut the lines that supply water to the community, and as a result Minago has experienced a serious outbreak of cholera.[276] Since water lines are a clear necessity for survival, their destruction constitutes a violation of the rules of war.

In a number of areas, civilians complained that the FDD compelled or intimidated people into providing shelter, food, and other supplies. An informant from Cibitoke told Human Rights Watch that FDD combatants required people in his area to support them. "The assailants kill many. If you don't give, they can kill

---

[273]Human Rights Watch interview, near Rumonge, Bururi, July 1, 1997.

[274]Human Rights Watch interviews in Bubanza, June 27, 1997.

[275]Human Rights Watch interview at Kizina, Bubanza, June 27, 1997.

[276]Human Rights Watch interviews in Minago, Bururi, July 1, 1997.

you. They ask for money."[277] A man in Bugenyuzi, Karuzi said that when the FDD was active in the area, they forced the population to support them. "When the assailants came and saw a nice house, they installed themselves there. They took food by force, stole chickens and other things."[278] Informants in Rutegama, Muramvya claimed that until military operations began in their area in October 1996, FDD soldiers often passed through and asked people to provide food. People did so out of fear that they might otherwise be killed. One man showed the Human Rights Watch research team several buildings which he said the FDD combatants had taken over for their own use.[279]

The Ministry of Defense reported in October 1997 that insurgent groups had burned seventeen primary schools in Bujumbura-Rural. The U.N. Human Rights Field Operation in Burundi confirmed in a November 1997 report that insurgent groups had begun a strategy of burning schools and farms.[280]

Restrictions on Movement

The FDD maintains at least nominal control over a number of small areas within Burundi, including parts of the Kibira Forest in Bubanza and Cibitoke, the highlands of the Congo-Nile continental divide in Bururi and Bujumbura-Rural, and Nyanza-Lac in Makamba. One of the most common accusations leveled by the government of Burundi against the FDD is that they have taken Hutu civilians hostage and forced them to live with them in their areas of control to provide farm labor. While Human Rights Watch was not able to visit FDD-controlled areas because of security concerns, evidence suggests that at least some civilians have in fact been compelled to remain under FDD control.

A number of informants in areas bordering FDD-controlled territory told Human Rights Watch that people are forced to live with the rebels. One severely malnourished woman said that her family had fled to Murwi Commune in Cibitoke when government soldiers attacked their community in Ndora in late 1995, killing members of her family and burning her home. She said that the FDD soldiers

---

[277]Human Rights Watch interviews in Muruta commune, Kayanza, June 24, 1997.

[278]Human Rights Watch interview near Bugenyuzi, Karuzi, June 13, 1997.

[279]Human Rights Watch interviews in Rutegama Commune, Muramvya, June 11, 1997.

[280]U.N. Department of Humanitarian Affairs, IRIN, "Emergency Update No. 288 on the Great Lakes," November 8-10, 1997; "Burundi Hutu Rebels Burn 17 Schools," Panafrican News Agency, October 22, 1997.

watched over the population and took whatever they could from them. "The assailants took all the harvest and beer that I had, all my pots and pans, everything."[281] Other people who told Human Rights Watch that they had fled from parts of Cibitoke where the FDD was active, if not clearly in control, suffered from severe malnutrition. From their testimonies, however, it is not clear to what extent they remained in these areas out of fear of the armed forces and to what extent because of compulsion from the FDD.[282]

A resident in Buteganzwa, Kayanza, near the Kibira Forest, told Human Rights Watch, "The assailants have taken some people hostage and forced them to go live in the forest and farm for them."[283] When pressed for examples, the witness mentioned the local communal administrator, Thadée, and the chief of Musema sector, Leonidas. However, he then allowed that these two had gone willingly to join the FDD. "Since the arrival of the new military governor, many administrators have fled to the CNDD out of fear."[284] He nevertheless insisted that there were periodically people who arrived in the regroupment camp where he lived who claimed that the FDD had coerced them to remain in the forest.

In January 1997, the Associated Press reported on interviews with Hutu in Bubanza who had lived under FDD control:

> For more than a year, Emmanuel Sibomana and his family were virtual hostages of Hutu rebels in the forested hills of northwest Burundi. They were forced to raise crops for the insurgents. When they didn't provide enough food and drink they were fined or beaten, although they, too, were Hutus and on the same side in Burundi's three-year civil war. ...
>
> "Life was very hard with the rebels," said Sibomana, thirty-seven, whose skin is bumpy with scabies. "They took everything from the fields and left us with nothing to eat. We couldn't leave for any reason—not to find food or medicine or anything."[285]

---

[281]Human Rights Watch interview in Muruta Commune, Kayanza, June 24, 1997.

[282]Human Rights Watch interviews in Muruta Commune, Kayanza, June 24, 1997.

[283]Human Rights Watch interview in Buteganzwa, Kayanza, June 23, 1997.

[284]Ibid.

[285]Karin Davies, "Hutus Flee Rebels, Shun Violence," Associated Press, January 31, 1997.

Without visiting the territory under FDD control, it is difficult to estimate what portion of the population lives there under compulsion. Interviews with people who have left Kibira suggest that fear of the Burundian armed forces is probably the greatest factor keeping civilians in the forest, but that the FDD combatants take advantage of civilians under their control, compelling them to labor on their behalf, even to the point of leaving the people without enough food to feed their families.[286] Sources in Bururi indicate that some people continue voluntarily to leave IDP and regroupment camps to return to their homes in areas of FDD control, but that others emerge from those areas claiming to have been coerced to remain in FDD controlled areas, and forced to farm.[287]

[286]Human Rights Watch interviews in Muruta, Kayanza, June 24, 1997.

[287]Human Rights Watch interviews in Bururi, June 20-21 and July 1, 1997.

VI. "WHEN TWO ELEPHANTS FIGHT...":
THE WAR AGAINST CIVILIAN POPULATIONS IN BURUNDI

In the extensive interviewing of Burundian civilians for this report, one message arose consistently in the testimonies: Civilians feel trapped between the two sides in the war. Since the conflict broke out in 1993, relatively few direct confrontations between government troops and rebel forces have taken place. Instead, both sides in the conflict have focused their attacks on the civilian population. Both sides have demanded support from civilians and have punished those who have refused to cooperate. Both sides have carried out indiscriminate attacks against unarmed civilians and have engaged in rape, torture, and extrajudicial executions (including assassinations). The civil war in Burundi has above all else been a war against civilians.

The proverb that one Burundian informant quoted to Human Rights Watch aptly expresses the tragic situation for Burundian civilians: "When two elephants fight, it is the grass that gets trampled."[288] As the armed forces of Burundi and the FDD vie for power, it is the unarmed civilian population that suffers.

Civilian Population Trapped in the Middle

People throughout Burundi told Human Rights Watch that they feel trapped between the two sides in the civil war. Both the armed forces of Burundi and rebel troops have killed and stolen from civilians, and the people repeatedly said that they fear both sides. Many people said that they felt caught in a tragic dilemma: if they support the FDD, they can be targeted by the government for retaliation, but if they refuse to support the FDD, they can be targeted by the FDD. What one person in Karuzi told us seemed to express a general sentiment: "We don't trust anyone, neither side, neither the soldiers nor the assailants."[289]

The typical pattern of violence in Burundi has consisted of an attack on some (usually civilian) target by one side, followed by a retaliatory attack by the other, almost invariably directed at civilians. When the FDD has attacked military posts and killed soldiers, the army has responded by killing Hutu civilians. When the army has attempted to assert its control over an area, the FDD has responded by ambushing vehicles. As one expatriate who has lived in Burundi throughout the conflict told Human Rights Watch, "It is always the same. The assailants come and

---

[288]Human Rights Watch interview, Bururi, July 1, 1997.

[289]Human Rights Watch interview, Bihemba, Bugenyuzi, Karuzi, June 13, 1997.

steal cows and other things. Then the soldiers come and burn the houses and kill people."[290]

A number of attacks by the armed forces detailed in chapter four were in retaliation for FDD strikes. This type of attack and counter-attack has been experienced throughout the country. A person in Bururi told Human Rights Watch, "In May, the rebels passed above and below this spot. They stole many cows. In the end, there were some dead and injured by the rebels, but very few. The military have been responsible for the overwhelming number of killings. The military always kills civilians."[291]

The weekend of July 12-13, 1997, the army and the FDD killed twenty civilians in fighting and afterwards in Kabezi, a town just south of the capital in Bujumbura-Rural. According to witnesses sited in a Reuters report, the FDD attacked Kabezi center on the night of July 12, killing four people. They killed two others nearby. Other witnesses said that the army had killed other civilians, because they accused the civilian population of supporting the FDD.[292]

An informant from Magara, a town on Lake Tanganyika about forty kilometers south of Bujumbura told Human Rights Watch, "In February 1997, the military took the chief of a hill from Magara. They took him to the military post at Gataza and killed him. On February 17, the rebels came and took the chief of Magara Zone and killed him in his home. They said it was a response. We could not understand anymore. One side kills and the other kills, what is that?"[293] After the FDD assassination of the chief of Magara Zone, the military forced the population of the area into a regroupment camp for a month as punishment for the FDD action.

Many people told Human Rights Watch that even when the possibility presented itself, the army rarely confronted the rebels directly. Armed forces took five hours to arrive at Buta, which is only ten minutes from Bururi, an important garrison town. When the FDD attacked the Catholic center at Kiryama, soldiers took forty minutes to respond, although their post is only a few hundred meters away.[294] People told Human Rights Watch, "You never hear of direct battles. It

---

[290]Human Rights Watch interview, Bujumbura, June 15, 1997.

[291]Human Rights Watch interview, Bururi, June 21, 1997.

[292]"More than 70 reported killed in Burundi," Reuters, July 17, 1997.

[293]Human Rights Watch interview, Bujumbura-Rural, June 28, 1997.

[294]Human Rights Watch interviews, Bururi, June 20, 1997.

is always the assailants coming down to steal, which they have to do to survive, and then the army comes in and attacks the population. They never get the rebels. They always kill the civilians."[295]

The threat of attacks from both sides in the conflict leaves the civilian population feeling trapped. The situation described to Human Rights Watch by residents of Mpira sector of Muramvya was typical for Hutu in many parts of the country. According to them, the armed forces killed a large number of people when they set up regroupment camps beginning in October 1996. According to one man, "When the attack started, we went into the forest to hide. We spent many days in the hills, many, many. Now there are no blankets, no food. Everything was stolen or burned."[296] Everyone in the group of fifteen men interviewed by Human Rights Watch had someone in their immediate family killed by the armed forces. One older man lost his son, aged twenty-five. Another lost his father, aged seventy-five, his older brother, aged forty-five, his uncle, aged sixty, and his cousin, aged thirty-five. Another lost his brother, aged forty.[297]

Despite this persecution by government troops, the crowd of Hutu informants did not enthusiastically support the CNDD. Instead, they claimed that they had also suffered when the FDD was active in the area:

> There was a period when there was infiltration by the rebels. We heard the exchange of gunfire. The rebels asked for food by force. If you did not give it, you would be killed. We have two problems—we have a fear of the army and a fear of the assailants. They [the rebels] demanded food, then cattle. Then they killed, even if you gave them what they asked for. If you did not have the same ideology as them, they would kill you.[298]

As examples of those killed by the rebels, they mentioned Venerant Nzibindavyi, aged forty-five, Mbunuza, aged fifty-five, and Gaspar Ntifihizina, aged thirty-five,

---

[295]Human Rights Watch interview, Bujumbura, June 15, 1997.

[296]Human Rights Watch interview, Mushikamo zone, Rutegama, Muramvya, June 11, 1997.

[297]Human Rights Watch interviews, Mushikamo zone, Rutegama, Muramvya, June 11, 1997.

[298]Human Rights Watch interview, Mushikamo zone, Rutegama, Muramvya, June 11, 1997.

all Hutu men. The population feared both sides in the conflict and felt constrained by the dual threats leveled against them by the armed forces and the FDD.

People from Cibitoke explained to Human Rights Watch that they were similarly targeted by both the army and the rebels. Several women interviewed at a health center in Kayanza reported that the FDD came at night and attacked people who lived in government-controlled areas or whom they believed supported the government. They stole from these people and sometimes killed them. Soldiers then came in the day and attacked those civilians "who were not with them," who lived in areas controlled by the FDD or whom they believed to be FDD supporters.[299]

One resident in Bururi told Human Rights Watch, "There is pillaging during the night and pillaging during the day, but it is done by different actors. In the day it is the soldiers, and at night it is the assailants.... The assailants are at about the same level as the military. They threaten people, demand money and food. They take young people to join their ranks."[300]

A series of attacks on Bujumbura's northern suburbs in the first week of 1998 aptly demonstrate the pattern of attack and counter-attack that traps the civilian population. From 3 a.m. to 8 a.m. on New Year's morning, FDD troops attacked the Bujumbura airport and the nearby Gakumbu military camp with heavy mortar fire. The fighting killed several hundred civilians who were trapped between the army and the rebels in the village of Rukaramu. Both the army and the CNDD denied responsibility for the civilian deaths.[301] In the aftermath of the attack, 7,000 civilians fled the region around the airport, many of them to the nearby community of Maramvya. On January 6, 1998, the FDD attacked the military base at Maramvya, driving an estimated 8,000 people into Bujumbura, including 3,000 who had earlier fled Rukaramu. During the next week, the armed forces attacked the region north of Bujumbura using helicopter gunships and aircraft fitted with

---

[299]Human Rights Watch interview, Muruta commune, Kayanza, June 24, 1997.

[300]Human Rights Watch interview, Bururi, June 21, 1997.

[301]"Burundi capital hit in New Year's Eve attack," Agence France Presse, January 1, 1998; "Burundi: Rebel Spokesman: Airport Attack Lesson to Arms Traffickers," La Une Radio Network, January 2, 1998; U.N. Department of Humanitarian Affairs, IRIN, "Update No. 324 for Central and Eastern Africa," January 2, 1998.

rockets to drive rebels out of the region, leading to an undetermined number of casualties.[302]

The creation of regroupment camps created a particular dilemma for the Hutu civilian population. As one source told Human Rights Watch:

> In certain communes, people were afraid of the military but also of the FDD. The FDD said, "If you go into the camps, we will shoot you." Then the military came and said, "If you do not go in two days, we will kill you." So some people stayed in their homes, because they said that they would be killed anyway, and they would rather die in their homes.[303]

In many cases, people are not even clear which side attacked them. One woman from Rugano in Cibitoke told Human Rights Watch, "We were attacked, but we don't know by whom. They wore military boots, though not everyone. And some people had on military uniforms." After the attack, her family and others in the community fled into the forest. Three members of her family were killed by gunshot wounds, and six have died of starvation or disease. When asked why she did not simply go home, she responded, "No one is living at home in my area. The military is always looking to drive us away."[304]

At a small commercial center that had been completely gutted by fire in Kigamba, Makamba, witnesses told Human Rights Watch that they did not know which side had burned the buildings. The attack had occurred in May 1997, at a time when people were spending the nights hiding outdoors because of insecurity. "It was during the night, while there was rain. We could not see who did it, because we were hiding in the marsh. It was about 2 a.m. on a Thursday, and we saw the buildings burning."[305] Following this attack, the population in the area fled to Nyankara, Kayogoro, and Mubera, and when they returned, they found many

---

[302]"Civilians flee as Burundian army mops up after rebel attack," Agence France Presse, January 3, 1998; U.N. Department of Humanitarian Affairs, IRIN, "Update No. 326 for Central and Eastern Africa," January 6, 1998; "15 Burundian rebels killed in raid: army," Agence France Presse, January 6, 1998; "More than 50 killed in Burundi fighting," CNN, January 12, 1998.

[303]Human Rights Watch interview, Bujumbura, June 6, 1997.

[304]Human Rights Watch interview, Muruta commune, Kayanza, June 24, 1997.

[305]Human Rights Watch interviews, Kigamba zone, Kayogoro, Makamba, June 19, 1997.

homes burned, but because they were not present, they claimed they did not know who was responsible.[306]

Disruptions Caused by the War

The consistent targeting of civilians by all sides in the conflict in Burundi has had a profoundly detrimental cumulative effect on the population. Families are slowly thinned as one family member after another disappears or is shot dead or dies of disease. Those who survive become increasingly exhausted and disheartened as they feel trapped in the middle of the conflict with no possible refuge.

One result of the war has been a massive displacement of people. The fighting has driven hundreds of thousands of Burundians to seek refuge either inside Burundi or in neighboring countries. An estimated 350,000 Tutsi are living in IDP (internally displaced people) camps throughout the country. While some Hutu are also in IDP camps, such as those in and around Bujumbura, many other Hutu are scattered throughout the country, living with extended family or seeking shelter wherever they are able. Relief workers in Bujumbura-Rural report that they work with many families who fled from Cibitoke and Bubanza early in the war, when fighting was focused there, and who became trapped in the countryside around Bujumbura when the fighting expanded into that area. They cannot go home, because of continued fighting, yet they also face insecurity where they are now sheltered and they have little access to food and health care.[307] In some cases, as discussed in chapter four, the Burundian government has forced Hutu out of IDP camps and back to their homes, where they have been exposed to the danger of indiscriminate attacks, summary execution, and other threats.

Since the beginning of the civil war, many Hutu have fled Burundi for refuge in Rwanda, Tanzania, and the Democratic Republic of the Congo (formerly Zaire). Some 230,000 Burundians have been sheltered in camps in Tanzania and another 200,000 in the ex-Zaire.[308] However, refugees have been driven out of each of these countries. A number of Burundian Hutu refugees were involved in the genocide in Rwanda in 1994, and when the largely Tutsi Rwandan Patriotic Front took control of Rwanda, Burundian Hutu fled Rwanda for Tanzania, Zaire, or back

---

[306]Human Rights Watch interviews, Kigamba zone, Kayogoro, Makamba, June 19, 1997.

[307]Human Rights Watch interviews in Bujumbura, June 15, 1997.

[308]United Nations Department of Humanitarian Affairs, Integrated Regional Information Network, "Emergency Update on the Great Lakes," no. 85, January 23, 1997.

into Burundi. When the Alliance of Democratic Forces for the Liberation of Congo-Zaire (ADFL) began the campaign which eventually ousted President Mobutu and installed Laurent Kabila as the new president, they targeted refugee camps in South Kivu where both Rwandan and Burundian Hutu were living, driving thousands of Burundian Hutu either deeper into Zaire or back into Burundi.[309] In late 1996 and again in late 1997, Tanzania also closed refugee camps. While these camps housed primarily Rwandan refugees, the Tanzanian government also forced home thousands of Burundian refugees.

In some cases, people have been driven from one place to another in search of refuge. Hutu living in Gahongore Regroupment Camp south of Bubanza town told Human Rights Watch how they had fled time after time to escape violence. People had been living at home in their communities in Mpanda commune when the Burundi army attacked in June and July 1996, killing a number of civilians and prompting the survivors to flee into Zaire. Then in October and November 1996, the ADFL attacked the refugee camps in Uvira and Fizi, Zaire, killing many more people. The Hutu civilians who survived those attacks then fled back into Burundi, and once across the border, the Burundian army once again attacked them and killed people. The survivors settled briefly in camps near the Zaire border, before being transported back to their home province, Bubanza. Now in the camp, people do not have access to their fields because of insecurity, and water supplies are inadequate, so people are dying of starvation and disease.[310]

The persistent displacement of the population has created a troubling humanitarian situation. Without access to their fields, people have few options for finding food to feed their families. In Kayanza, many people who had fled from Cibitoke to seek treatment for malnutrition told Human Rights Watch that they had been living with host families or in makeshift refugee camps in the forest. One woman suffering from severe malnutrition said that she had been living in the forest for more than two years, since soldiers attacked and burned her home and killed her father-in-law, brother-in-law, and others.[311] Another severely malnourished man said that he had fled his community in Masango a year earlier and had been living with a family. "But because of poverty, there is nothing to

---

[309]For a more detailed account of the targeting of refugees, see Human Rights Watch and the International Federation of Human Rights Leagues, "Attacked by All Sides: Civilians and the War in Eastern Zaire," March 1997.

[310]Human Rights Watch interviews, Gahongore, Bubanza, June 27, 1997.

[311]Human Rights Watch interview, Muruta commune, Kayanza, June 24, 1997.

eat." The three-and-a-half year old daughter with him was covered with scabies and sores. Her legs and feet and hands were badly swollen from lack of protein. He himself had lost much of his hair and was emaciated so that, although he was twenty-three, he looked much younger.[312]

This child is suffering from severe malnutrition and scabies as a result of long-term displacement of his family due to instability.

Medical and relief workers have encountered similar situations in Bujumbura-Rural and Bururi, as people who have suffered from long-term displacement come seeking help when it is almost too late. Action Contre la Faim (ACF), which runs a feeding center at Maramvya, reported in August 1997 that some twenty people were dying each week from malnutrition, mostly refugees from Bubanza and Cibitoke.[313] In November 1997, the U.N. Department of Humanitarian Affairs reported that 46,000 children were registered for therapeutic or supplementary

[312]Human Rights Watch interview, Muruta commune, Kayanza, June 24, 1997.

[313]United Nations Department of Humanitarian Affairs, Integrated Regional Information Network, "IRIN Weekly Roundup 18-97 of Main Events in the Great Lakes region, covering the period 19-25 August 1997," August 25, 1997.

feeding in Burundi, far beyond the capacities of the country's feeding centers.[314] A medical worker in Bujumbura-Rural told Human Rights Watch that so many people were dying of hunger that they were running out of places to bury them. She was struck by one group of twelve bodies that she saw in early June 1997. "They died as they had lived, completely abandoned. Their eyes were open, because no one was there who cared enough to close their eyes. They are like ghosts, skin and bone."[315]

The problems arising from the war are not restricted to Hutu. As the civil war persists, displaced Tutsi feel increasingly frustrated. Many displaced Tutsi have been in the camps since the massacres that shook the country after President Ndadaye's assassination in 1993.

Human Rights Watch visited camps for the internally displaced in Muramvya, Gitega, Ruyigi, Ngozi, Kayanza, and Makamba and found the residents expressing growing frustration. Tutsi in the IDP camps told Human Rights Watch that they do not feel safe to return to their homes and that they see little hope of security improving to the point that they will be able to return to their homes in the foreseeable future. According to the governor of Gitega, these fears are probably justified, since a group of Tutsi who were forced to return to their homes in Gitega in 1995 were subsequently killed.[316] In some provinces, such as Karuzi, the Tutsi population was so devastated by the violence in 1993 that their numbers are now minimal.[317] The displaced Tutsi expressed serious frustration and anger at the continued disruption of their lives. At the same time, it is important to note that the Tutsi IDP camps have received privileged treatment from the government. Compared to the regroupment camps, the IDP are relatively well supplied and well protected. Housing is more spacious, and malnutrition and disease do not appear to be serious problems.

The persistence of the conflict in Burundi has created a cycle of interethnic tension. Hutu become frustrated at the continuing human rights abuses directed against them and may respond, as they have at various times in recent history, by

---

[314]U.N. Department of Humanitarian Affairs, IRIN, "Emergency Update No. 285 on the Great Lakes," November 5, 1997.

[315]Human Rights Watch interview, Bujumbura, June, 1997.

[316]Colonel Murengera, Governor of Gitega, Human Rights Watch interview, Gitega, June 14, 1997.

[317]Human Rights Watch interviews, Karuzi, June 13, 1997.

attacking Tutsi civilians. Tutsi civilians, feeling insecure, encourage the armed forces to repress the Hutu more forcefully. The result is that in most of the country, both groups live in fear of one another. While Human Rights Watch did encounter some multi-ethnic communities in Gitega, Bururi, and Makamba, interethnic tensions in these areas remained high. Only in Bujumbura, where very few Hutu remain, do Tutsi feel generally safe, and many Tutsi residents of Bujumbura are afraid to leave the city.

The civilian population seems to move from one tragedy to the next. One man from Gashanga told Human Rights Watch that he was injured by gunfire before he fled to Zaire. "I was with a group of twenty people, and the soldiers attacked, looking for assailants. They fired and we ran. I was shot, but I kept running. I saw six people dead along the path as I went. I fled to Zaire to get treatment."[318] Because of his injuries, he lost his hand. He fled Zaire when the ADFL attacked his camp, stayed in Cibitoke briefly, then arrived in Bubanza in February 1997.

In one commune in Bururi, the communal high school had 250 students before Easter, but after Easter break, less than one hundred returned. Attendance at the local health center has also plummeted.[319] Education and health care have been disrupted throughout much of the country.

Landmines

One factor that has contributed to the deteriorating situation for the civilian population in Burundi is the use of antipersonnel and antitank landmines, which has increased substantially over the past year, leading to a growing number of civilian deaths and injuries. No side in the conflict in Burundi admits to using landmines. Army spokesman Colonel Nibizi told Human Rights Watch that the Burundian armed forces never use landmines, "because they kill innocent people."[320] Nevertheless, an increasing number of civilians have been killed or injured by landmines since the beginning of the year, and there is reason to believe that all sides in the conflict may have used landmines.

Human Rights Watch spoke with a number of people in Bubanza hospital who were injured by landmines, including several young children. Most mine victims were from Musigati, a regroupment camp near the Kibira Forest, but mines have

---

[318]Human Rights Watch interviews, Gahongore, Bubanza, June 27, 1997.

[319]Human Rights Watch interview, Bururi, June 21, 1997.

[320]Col. Isaie Nibizi, Army Spokesman, Human Rights Watch interview, Bujumbura, June 27, 1997.

also taken a toll in Ngara and in other parts of Bubanza. Those hospitalized for mine-related injuries reported that mines are triggered on a nearly daily basis around the Bubanza regroupment camps.[321]

Mine incidents have been increasing in other parts of the country as well. The following are a sample of mine incidents in 1997 and 1998:

- On January 12, 1998, two people were injured when their vehicle, owned by the international NGO Action Internationale Contre le Faim (AICF), hit a mine in Maramvya, Bujumbura-Rural, near the Bujumbura airport.[322]

- Nine people were killed and forty-seven wounded when a truck hit a landmine near the Teza tea plantation on October 27, 1997.[323]

- Six people were killed when a minibus belonging to an international NGO detonated a landmine on a dirt road in Gihanga commune, Bubanza, in October 1997.[324]

- Twelve people were killed and five injured on August 17, 1997, when the minibus they were riding in hit an antitank mine on the Lake Tanganyika road between Rumonge and Bujumbura.[325]

- An antitank mine near Ndava in Cibitoke killed nine people in a minibus on August 4, 1997.[326]

---

[321]Human Rights Watch interviews, Bubanza, June 27, 1997.

[322]"Un vehicule de l'AICF Saute sur une Mine Anti-Char," Net Press, January 15, 1998.

[323]U.N. Department of Humanitarian Affairs, IRIN, "Emergency Update No. 279 on the Great Lakes," October 28, 1997.

[324]U.N. Department of Humanitarian Affairs, IRIN, "Emergency Update No. 271 on the Great Lakes," October 16, 1997.

[325]Panafrican News Agency, "Twelve Die in Burundi Mine Explosion," August 18, 1997.

[326]United Nations Department of Humanitarian Affairs, "Humanitarian Situation Report," July 31-August 6, 1997.

- The wife of the parliamentary speaker, Léonce Ngendakumana, was injured and her bodyguard killed on July 1, 1997, when her vehicle hit a mine near her home. While presumedly not directly targeted at the speaker's wife, the mine was planted on a street where many Frodebu officials live.[327]

- In March, April, and May 1997, a number of mine incidents occurred in Bujumbura. Burundi state radio reported that seven people were killed by landmines in Bujumbura on March 12, 1997.[328]

Mine warfare appears to have been carried out by different parties in the conflict in different areas. Mine laying in Bujumbura has been widely attributed to Tutsi forces loyal to former president Bagaza who wanted to undermine Buyoya and to protest involvement in talks with the FDD. The military spokesman told Agence France Presse "we have reason to believe that the mines were planted by [Bagaza's political party] PARENA,"[329] and diplomatic and other sources concur with this assessment.

Mines on the Lake Tanganyika road seem consistent with the FDD's strategy of discouraging commerce and undermining economic activity, which has included ambushes of vehicles. Human Rights Watch researchers traveled along this road and can attest to the ease with which FDD combatants would be able to operate freely in the area because of forest cover and the isolation of the area.

Finally, government troops seem to have the strongest motives for using landmines in Bubanza and Cibitoke. A number of government officials told Human Rights Watch that the FDD passed across northern Burundi from Tanzania to the Democratic Republic of the Congo (DRC) along a corridor that includes Bubanza and Cibitoke. Since the Kibira Forest is acknowledged to be an important base for the FDD, laying mines in Bubanza and Cibitoke could serve to cut off the passage of the FDD from Kibiria to the DRC.

In September 1997, the Tanzanian government accused the Burundian military of planting mines along their mutual border in Makamba. According to the Tanzanian Home Affairs Minister Ali Amir Mohamed, the mining of the border is

---

[327]Human Rights Watch interviews, Bujumbura, July 2, 1997.

[328]Cited in United Nations Department of Humanitarian Affairs, Integrated Regional Information Network, "Emergency Update on the Great Lakes," no. 127, March 13, 1997.

[329]Cited in United Nations Department of Humanitarian Affairs, Integrated Regional Information Network, "Emergency Update on the Great Lakes," no. 127, March 13, 1997.

a response to fighting in the region and has disrupted the voluntary repatriation of Burundian refugees. Refugees who continue to flee into Tanzania to escape continued fighting in Southern Burundi are vulnerable to the mines. A Burundian who fled to Tanzania described in a Voice of America interview how one of the people fleeing Burundi with him stepped on a mine and was killed: "The rest of us were hurt, but we kept walking slowly, slowly towards the border . . . Everywhere you try to go there are bombs . . . even the small paths."[330]

Burundi is one of the 123 governments that signed the Convention on the Prohibition of the Use, Stockpiling, Production and Transfer of Anti-Personnel Mines and On Their Destruction in Ottawa, Canada in December 1997. This comprehensive treaty prohibits in all circumstances any use of antipersonnel landmines. It also requires that stockpiles be destroyed within four years of the treaty's entry into force, and that mines already in the ground be removed and destroyed within ten years.

It is an established principle of international law that a state is obliged to refrain from acts which would defeat the object and purpose of a treaty it has signed pending that treaty's ratification or entry into force.[331]

This treaty does not provide for any restrictions or prohibitions on antitank mines. However, it appears that many uses of antitank mines in Burundi have been in violation of the prohibitions on indiscriminate attacks on civilians contained in customary international humanitarian law and in the 1977 Protocols Additional to the Geneva Conventions of 1949.

Human Rights Watch calls on the government of Burundi to ratify the ban treaty as soon as possible, and to abide by the treaty until that time. Human Rights Watch believes that the use of antipersonnel landmines by all parties to the conflict is already banned under the provisions of customary international humanitarian law that protect civilians from indiscriminate attack and that mandate that parties to a conflict weigh the expected military utility of a weapon against the anticipated human toll.[332]

---

[330]Scott Stearns, "Burundi Land Mines," Voice of America, September 11, 1997.

[331]This is set forth in the Vienna Convention of the Law of Treaties, Article 18.

[332]For a detailed legal analysis of the use of antipersonnel landmines, see *Landmines: A Deadly Legacy* (New York: Human Rights Watch, 1993), pp. 261-318.

VII. MILITARIZATION OF BURUNDIAN SOCIETY

The lack of ethnic integration in the Burundian armed forces has been a major barrier to a peaceful settlement of the ongoing conflict in Burundi. The armed forces, which are the most powerful institution in Burundian society, are overwhelmingly Tutsi, and they have long considered protecting the interests and safety of the Tutsi minority their fundamental responsibility.

During his first term as president from 1987-93, Buyoya earned international praise for bringing Hutu into the government, then peacefully relinquishing power to the Hutu candidate who won the multiparty elections in June 1993. Buyoya's failure to bring Hutu into the armed forces, however, doomed the democratic transition. Much of the Tutsi public, including many military officers and soldiers, opposed any transfer of power to the Hutu, believing it would ultimately lead to their annihilation, and they used the armed forces as a basis for undermining efforts to establish a stable democracy. A group of soldiers assassinated President Ndadaye in October 1993, but failed to receive sufficient support from the military and the international community to sustain their coup. Over the next three years, however, the armed forces thwarted the civilian government's attempts to establish order by supporting Tutsi civilian militia and youth gangs, assassinating Hutu and some moderate Tutsi politicians, and massacring Hutu civilians. Although the presidents who succeeded Ndadaye were themselves Hutu, the largely Hutu National Coalition for the Defense of Democracy (CNDD) took up arms in 1993, claiming that Hutu would never enjoy civil and political rights until they controlled the armed forces.

The issue of ethnic balance in the armed forces remains a major matter of contention between the CNDD and the Buyoya regime. Research by Human Rights Watch reveals that the since the July 1996 coup, the Tutsi dominance of the armed forces has been exacerbated by a massive recruitment of new soldiers. In order to expand the recruiting base for troops without including Hutu, the armed forces have brought women into the gendarmerie and have recruited an increasing number of child soldiers. According to some testimonies, the military is now recruiting boys as young as ten. The armed forces have also been training Tutsi civilian militia and distributing arms to Tutsi civilians. While not bringing Hutu into positions where they might have access to firearms, the military has organized Hutu men in much of the country into groups that patrol their communities, allowing the military to monitor the Hutu population, restricting freedom of movement, and preventing people from supporting the FDD. The government has also implicated the Hutu population in the war effort by levying an onerous war tax. The government and armed forces seem intent on maintaining Tutsi dominance over Hutu through military means.

109

Massive Expansion of the Armed Forces

In its recent research visit to Burundi, Human Rights Watch found that in addition to the extensive acquisition of arms by both sides in the civil war, the armed forces of Burundi have undertaken a massive expansion of personnel. According to diplomatic sources, the military has increased in size since the July 1996 coup from around 20,000 to more than 40,000.[333] The armed forces has recruited gang members, students, children, and many others, but, as even the military spokesman admits, the new soldiers are almost exclusively Tutsi.

One major source of new recruits for the armed forces has been the Tutsi youth gangs. Following the assassination of Ndadaye, rival Hutu and Tutsi youth gangs emerged, particularly in Bujumbura, and engaged in gang warfare. With logistical and material support from the armed forces, the Tutsi militia such as the Sans Echec and Sans Défaite dominated the inter-gang conflict. They terrorized the Hutu population in and around Bujumbura in 1994 and 1995, robbing, raping, and destroying homes, and eventually forcing most Hutu to flee the city. Prior to the July 1996 coup, the gang violence served the purposes of those Tutsi who supported a return to military rule by contributing to insecurity in the country that could be used to justify military intervention. Following the coup, however, the new military government wanted to bring the gangs under control, as well as increase the size of the military, and so they conscripted several thousand gang members into the armed forces.[334]

Another source of new recruits for the armed forces has been students. The government has implemented a national service requirement for all students finishing secondary school, which has so far provided around 4,000 recruits. According to the army spokesman, the students will serve on active duty for one year, then become military reservists.[335] Female students have been included in the conscription and have trained as gendarmes and assigned to control traffic, run roadblocks, and maintain order, primarily in the capital. As one diplomat told Human Rights Watch, "The women gendarmes allow the military to pull [male soldiers] out of Bujumbura and deploy them elsewhere in the country."[336]

---

[333]Human Rights Watch interview, June 7, 1997.

[334]Human Rights Watch interviews, June 1997.

[335]Human Rights Watch interview with Isaie Nibizi, Bujumbura, June 27, 1997.

[336]Human Rights Watch interview, June 7, 1997.

Furthermore, students have been a continuing source of political protest, and military service allows the government to keep them more effectively under control. Nearly all of the students conscripted have been Tutsi, both because many Hutu have been driven out of the schools and because the conscription was done selectively.

Several aspects of the military expansion are particularly troubling. The expansion has focused entirely on recruiting Tutsi, serving to further exaggerate the Tutsi dominance of the armed forces. Colonel Isaie Nibizi, the spokesman for the armed forces, told Human Rights Watch that the new recruits have been almost entirely Tutsi, but that "We have done everything in our power to recruit Hutu, but without very good results. We have been disappointed. This needs to be addressed."[337] Human Rights Watch found no evidence that attempts to recruit Hutu had in fact been made. In fact, according to sources in the capital, the armed forces clearly chose to conscript members of Tutsi and not Hutu gangs and Tutsi, not Hutu, students.

The new recruits are given very limited training. According to Col. Nibizi, the period for military training has been reduced from one year to three months.[338] With so many new recruits, the officer corps is stretched thin. According to Nibizi, "Because of the crisis, it is now often necessary to give low-ranking soldiers authority, maybe four or five people at a post with no officer."[339] Posting young soldiers with inadequate training and inadequate supervision creates a situation in which undisciplined behavior is easily tolerated. Despite official regulations limiting active duty officers to one beer per day, Human Rights Watch encountered numerous instances of heavy drinking by soldiers on duty, a situation which many informants linked to abusive behavior. In one regroupment camp in Karuzi, the official camp leaders, who are generally reluctant to criticize the military authorities openly, told Human Rights Watch, "We only have problems with soldiers when they are drunk. Then we flee."[340] Human Rights Watch observed visibly intoxicated soldiers in that camp and most others visited, suggesting a widespread problem.

---

[337]Human Rights Watch interview, Bujumbura, June 27, 1997.

[338]Human Rights Watch interview, Bujumbura, June 27, 1997.

[339]Human Rights Watch interview, Bujumbura, June 27, 1997.

[340]Human Rights Watch interview, Karuzi, June 13, 1997.

Guns prepared with rounds of ammunition and empty beer bottles are
a common sight at any military post.

The problem of limited training and insufficient supervision is particularly
acute given the conscription of gang members. Some diplomatic sources told
Human Rights Watch that the recruitment of the Tutsi gang members was a
potentially positive step which could bring them under control by instilling them
with military discipline, but the reduction in time for training means that gang
members receive only rudimentary instruction before being armed and assigned to
positions of authority. Many other sources attributed human rights abuses to the
continuing indiscipline of the former gang members—attributed in part to the short
period of training. Several Hutu sources pointed out that by placing the former
gang members as guards in regroupment camps and elsewhere, the new soldiers are
being charged with guarding the very people whom they had previously terrorized.
In many locations, soldiers receive very little supervision, and informants told
Human Rights Watch that the young soldiers were frequently involved in rape,
robbery, and other violations against Hutu civilians.

Moves by both the government and the CNDD to expand their weapons
arsenals and to recruit thousands of new troops suggest that both sides are hoping
for a military solution to the ongoing conflict. As one Frodebu official told Human
Rights Watch, "For four years they have raised the defense budget. But arms are
not going to bring peace to Burundi. They raise the defense budgets, but the war
does not stop. The more they recruit people into the military, the more the other

side recruits."[341]   Another Hutu politician told Human Rights Watch that while the army has conscripted Tutsi students, around 800 Hutu university students have joined the FDD.[342]

Child Soldiers

In their efforts at rapid expansion, the armed forces have recruited an increasing number of child soldiers. The official age for military service in Burundi is sixteen. During their travels through Burundi, however, Human Rights Watch researchers saw numerous soldiers who were younger than sixteen, including some who may have been as young as eleven or twelve who were armed and in uniform. Human Rights Watch saw children both in uniform on active duty and among new recruits being trained as soldiers or gendarmes. Other witnesses, both expatriate and Burundian, reported similar observations. One church worker told Human Rights Watch, "I have seen *gamins*, children of twelve or thirteen, just out of grade school, being trained at Kamenge. I have seen them marching."[343]

Human Rights Watch believes that children under the age of eighteen should not take part directly or indirectly in armed conflict.[344]   Under the rules of war (Protocol II to the 1949 Geneva Conventions), recruitment, voluntary or involuntary, of soldiers under the age of fifteen is illegal. Under the Convention on the Rights of the Child, ratified by Burundi on October 19, 1990, those who recruit soldiers between the ages of fifteen and eighteen must endeavor to give priority to those who are the oldest.[345]

One young soldier, a former member of the Tutsi youth gang Sans Echec, told Human Rights Watch that he was the eldest of four brothers, all of whom were in the military. When asked the minimum age at which recruits were accepted, he replied, "They are accepting boys of ten now."[346]   While this response does not prove an official policy of recruiting ten-year-olds, the spontaneity of the response

---

[341]Human Rights Watch interview, Bujumbura, June 25, 1997.

[342]Human Rights Watch interview, Bujumbura, June 16, 1997.

[343]Human Rights Watch interview in Bujumbura, June 15, 1997.

[344]See, Human Rights Watch, "Children in Combat," vol. 8, no. 1(G), January 1996.

[345]Convention on the Rights of the Child, art. 38(3).

[346]Human Rights Watch interview in Makamba, June 18, 1997.

suggested at least that members of the armed forces themselves have the impression that children as young as ten are being recruited. A group of high school age students in Vugizo, Makamba, told Human Rights Watch that there were soldiers as young as twelve and fourteen posted in their commune, though one student assured the research team that "the majority of soldiers are adults."[347]

Military Training of Tutsi Civilians and the Distribution of Arms

In addition to doubling the number of troops and extensively importing armaments, the armed forces have sought to bolster the military power of the Tutsi minority by offering military training to Tutsi civilians and providing them with arms. The military training and distribution of guns to civilians began in May and June 1997, apparently in response to the substantial FDD assault in the south, in which the FDD was able to expand the territory under their control in Bururi and Makamba and to penetrate into Rutovu commune, the very heart of Bururi, the home province of President Buyoya.

Military training of Tutsi civilians apparently began in Bujumbura during the first week of June 1997. One Tutsi source from Bujumbura told Human Rights Watch that military training for Tutsi was compulsory and was organized by neighborhood. The training, which he said was held on weekday afternoons from 4:30 to 6:30 p.m. and on Saturday mornings, focused on ideological training as well as knowledge of how to handle a gun. "Everyone has them [guns] in their homes, so we're learning how to use them."[348]

According to informants in Bururi, arms were distributed to Tutsi civilians in several communes in May 1997. According to one source, "They shoot twice, and that is their training."[349] In one community, the Tutsi grade school principal was given a gun, so the Hutu students have stopped attending class out of fear.[350] Sources reported having seen even civilian women carrying Kalishnikovs at a ceremony commemorating those massacred at Buta, Bururi. "It's a strategy of civil defense, but if they continue distributing arms to civilians, we will have another Rwanda. The military is not numerous enough, and they are counting on civilian

---

[347]Human Rights Watch interview, Vugizo, Makamba, June 19, 1997.

[348]Human Rights Watch interview, Bujumbura, June 6, 1997.

[349]Human Rights Watch interview in Bururi, June 21, 1997.

[350]Human Rights Watch interview in Bururi, June 21, 1997.

support for numbers." Other informants claim that the military is training and arming Tutsi civilians throughout the country.[351]

Military officials admit having begun military training for civilians, though they fall short of admitting distributing arms to civilians. Armed forces spokesperson Nibizi told Human Rights Watch, "In civil defense training, they are receiving a civic course, and how to use their arms. ... We have numerous problems here, and if there are some civilians who are armed and can fight off those acting uncivilly, the community will be the better for it. If there had been people prepared for civil defense at Teza [a tea factory in Bubanza that the FDD attacked and destroyed in 1996, killing a number of people], well, there might not have been a massacre."[352]

Bringing Hutu into the War Effort

In addition to bringing more Tutsi into the armed forces and arming civilian Tutsi in an effort to guarantee the continuing political and social dominance of the Tutsi group, the government and military leaders have sought to incorporate unarmed Hutu civilians in their war effort. By requiring Hutu to participate in patrols and pay a special war tax, the government and armed forces have used the Hutu population to assist in hindering FDD activity in the country and kept the Hutu civilians themselves under effective surveillance.

Informants in nearly every province in Burundi told Human Rights Watch that government officials or soldiers had organized nightly, and sometimes twenty-four hour, patrols. While the exact organization of the patrols is determined by local or provincial authorities, in most locations all adult Hutu men are required to assemble after dark in each neighborhood. In most areas, Tutsi men have not been required to participate in the patrols. Attendance is taken to ensure that everyone is present. The groups then spend the night patrolling their community to prevent strangers from passing through, sometimes accompanied by armed soldiers. Any unknown person encountered is arrested and taken to military or political authorities.[353]

---

[351]Human Rights Watch interview, Bujumbura, June 17, 1997.

[352]Human Rights Watch interview, Bujumbura, June 27, 1997.

[353]Human Rights Watch witnessed this process in action. In Kayanza, a patrol brought to the gendarmerie a man whose tattered clothing and state of malnutrition suggested that he had been living in a rebel-controlled area, although there was no indication that he was associated with the FDD and his ill-health would have prevented his being a combattant.

The minister of the interior, Colonel Epitace Bayaganakandi, admits that patrols have been instituted throughout much of the country: "When you need protection, you go out and buy a dog. Patrols are an initiative of the population. They want a means to protect themselves."[354] In fact, however, sources who participated in patrols regularly told Human Rights Watch that the government or armed forces had initiated the patrols. Many informants complained that the patrols were an onerous burden on their time, leaving them with no time to sleep and little energy for working their fields.

Participation in patrols is compulsory. As one Hutu man in Muramvya said, "You have to participate. The penalties for resisting are serious."[355] One man in Gitega reported "The men have to go on patrols every night. If you do not, you spend two months in prison and have a 5,000 franc fine."[356] People in Muramvya, Kayanza, and Karuzi said that those who failed to show up for the patrols were beaten or fined. They also risked being accused of working for the FDD, an accusation which often resulted in being arrested by the armed forces and summarily executed.

The patrols allow the armed forces to maintain close control over the Hutu population and to prevent them from developing contacts with the FDD and other rebel groups. Since every adult male must be accounted for in the patrols, men do not have the freedom to slip away at night and meet with FDD agents. By taking up a vast amount of their time, the patrols keep civilians too busy and tired to organize resistance. Furthermore, the military simplifies its job by enlisting Hutu to monitor themselves. Human Rights Watch witnessed at least one example of a Hutu patrol in Kayanza that turned over to local military authorities a Hutu man they had captured and arrested.

The government has also sought to force the civilian population, including Hutu, to support the war by implementing a war tax, called the Contribution to National Solidarity. A government decree issued in early June 1997 requires every family to pay 1,000 Burundian francs (about U.S. $3) per year.[357] This amount

---

[354]Colonel Epitace Bayaganakandi, Minister of the Interior, Human Rights Watch interview, Bujumbura, July 3, 1997.

[355]Human Rights Watch interview, Mpira sector, Rutegama zone, Muramvya, June 11, 1997.

[356]Human Rights Watch interview, Gitega, June 12, 1997.

[357]Human Rights Watch interview, June 30, 1997.

added onto existing tax bills is a heavy burden for families whose homes have been destroyed and who have virtually no means to raise funds.

The minister of the interior told Human Rights Watch, "The population needs to make an effort in this war. Those who are capable will be asked to contribute. The measure was taken globally, but it will not be asked of the regrouped and others who cannot pay. It was the population that asked for a way to support the war—not the people in bad conditions, but the businessmen, civil servants, peasants, because many of them do have the means."[358] Interviews with lower level government officials, however, indicate that the war tax is expected of all citizens, not simply those capable of paying. The concern expressed by some sources is that the implementation of the tax provides opportunities for officials to enforce the tax arbitrarily, levying disproportionate demands against those who cause problems or do not support them.

---

[358]Colonel Epitace Bayaganakandi, Minister of the Interior, Human Rights Watch interview, Bujumbura, July 3, 1997.

VIII. THE INTERNATIONAL RESPONSE

The Regional Context to the Conflict in Burundi

The civil war in Burundi cannot be fully understood without viewing it within a regional context. As in earlier periods of unrest, conflicts in recent years in neighboring countries have spilled over into Burundi, while the conflict in Burundi has reverberated across its borders. Any attempt to forge a solution to the Burundian civil war must take into account the wider regional situation.

Because of the similar ethnic compositions of Burundi and Rwanda, events in one country affect conditions in the other. The 1959 revolution that brought Hutu to power in Rwanda led Tutsi in Burundi to find ways to avoid a similar transfer of power in Burundi. The ethnic violence in Burundi in 1972 helped inspire a new outbreak of ethnic violence in Rwanda in 1973, which contributed to the fall of the Rwandan government in a coup later that year. The assassination of Ndadaye convinced many Hutu in Rwanda of the danger of compromising with the Tutsi, while the genocide in Rwanda convinced many Tutsi in Burundi of the dangers of allowing Hutu to wield power. Some Hutu who had fled Burundi during the 1993 violence played an active part in the genocide in Rwanda the next year.

The conflict in Burundi has also been affected by developments in the Democratic Republic of Congo, the former Zaire. The former armed forces of Rwanda (ex-FAR) and the Interahamwe militia who fled into Zaire and were based in refugee camps in Kivu province provided support to the FDD in its operations in Burundi. When the Alliance of Democratic Forces for the Liberation of Congo-Zaire (ADFL) began its campaign to drive President Mobutu from power, its troops targeted the camps of Rwandan and Burundian refugees and armed exiles, driving tens of thousands of Hutu back into Rwanda and Burundi. The armed forces of Burundi reportedly supported the ADFL in the civil war in Congo. Meanwhile, deprived of many of its bases in Congo, the FDD has apparently established new bases in Tanzania, straining relations between Burundi and Tanzania. Burundi has accused Tanzania of waging a campaign against Burundi by supporting the FDD and forcing other countries to accept sanctions against Burundi.[359]

In the international media and in diplomatic circles, the conflict in Burundi has been overshadowed by the genocide in Rwanda and by the civil war in Congo/Zaire. Given the inter-relatedness of these conflicts, however, such a continuing oversight could prove dangerous. Continued instability in Burundi has the potential to undermine security in the entire region.

---

[359]United Nations Department of Humanitarian Affairs, Integrated Regional Information Network, "Emergency Update on the Great Lakes," no. 231, August 19, 1997.

The Regional Reaction: Sanctions and Their Impact

Wary of the cross-border impact of events in Burundi, East African regional leaders took a strong stand against the military coup in Burundi. The heads of state of seven regional countries—Kenya, Tanzania, Ethiopia, Rwanda, Uganda, Zambia, and Zaire—gathered in Arusha a week after the July 1996 coup and issued a strong condemnation of the ouster of the civilian president. In an initiative apparently led by Ethiopia and Tanzania, the regional leaders leveled sanctions against Burundi and announced on July 31, 1996, that the borders of Burundi were to be closed.[360]

Over the course of the year after the embargo was imposed, the sanctions were eased somewhat. Due to humanitarian concerns, regional leaders eased the sanctions in April 1997, allowing the transport of food, construction materials, medicine, and agricultural items. At the same time, the leaders strongly condemned the regroupment camps and called for the government to create "a conducive spirit for national reconciliation and negotiations."[361] In July, both Kenya and the Democratic Republic of Congo announced that they were no longer going to participate in the sanctions.[362] But at a meeting in Arusha on September 4, 1997, the regional heads of state decided not only to maintain sanctions but to set up a secretariat to monitor their effectiveness.[363] The move was an apparent response to the Buyoya regime's last minute withdrawal from peace talks with the CNDD scheduled to begin on August 25. Representatives of groups which had come to Arusha for the scheduled talks were able to influence the gathered leaders and urge a maintenance of sanctions.[364] By the beginning of 1998, however, under pressure from international business interests, U.N. officials, and other states, the

---

[360]Barbara Crossette, "Rwanda Joins Effort to Isolate Burundi," *New York Times* August 9, 1997.

[361]"Sanctions Against Burundi Eased," Reuters, April 17, 1997.

[362]"Burundi: All Borders Between Burundi, DRCongo Reopened," Libreville Africa No. 1, July 16, 1997. Adonia Ayebare, "Ministers attack Kenya Embargo Breach," *East African*, August 18, 1997.

[363]"Burundi sanctions maintained," *New Vision* (Uganda), September 5, 1997.

[364]"Burundi Parties Exploit Buyoya's Arusha Meeting Boycott," *East African* September 3, 1997.

neighboring states appeared to be on the verge of moderating or perhaps eliminating the sanctions, provided Buyoya demonstrated a willingness to restart negotiations with the CNDD.[365]

The Impact of Sanctions

The impact of the sanctions on Burundian society has been mixed, but the issue of sanctions has proven to be a powerful motivator for the government. In Bujumbura, the main commercial center, most items are still available today, but at inflated prices. While gasoline is officially rationed, in practice it is abundantly available on the black market, albeit at a high price. As one expatriate told Human Rights Watch, "Traffic is as heavy in Bujumbura today as it was before the sanctions. The rich can find what they need."[366]

Concern was expressed to Human Rights Watch about the impact of the sanctions in the countryside and on common citizens. Several relief workers complained bitterly about the hardship that inflation and shortages had created for the rural poor. Some rural residents also complained about high prices. For example, when asked about the sanctions, one man who lives in Bihemba regroupment camp in Kayanza observed that, "We are poor. Before, we found cheap soap, but now we pay exorbitant prices. For clothes, too."[367] A World Health Organization and Food and Agriculture Organization study issued in July attributes the declining situation for food security at least in part to the sanctions.[368] The U.N. Special Rapporteur on Human Rights in Burundi, Paulo Sergio Pinheiro, called for an end to sanctions in his October 1997 report on human rights conditions Burundi because of the negative humanitarian consequences that he believed it was having.[369] Other observers, however, attribute problems of

---

[365]U.N. Department of Humanitarian Affairs, IRIN, "Weekly Round-up 32-97," November 21-27, 1997; U.N. Department of Humanitarian Affairs, IRIN, "Update No. 304 for Central and Eastern Africa," December 2, 1997.

[366]Human Rights Watch interview, Bujumbura, June 10, 1997.

[367]Human Rights Watch interview, Karuzi, June 13, 1997.

[368]Cited in United Nations Department of Humanitarian Affairs, Integrated Regional Information Network, "Weekly Roundup," no. 15-97, July 28-August 4, 1997.

[369]Paulo Sergio Pinheiro, Interim Report on the Human Rights Situation in Burundi (NewYork: United Nations, October 7, 1997), A/52/505.

shortages and malnutrition less to sanctions than to government policies such as regroupment, which have restricted access to fields, disrupted production, and destroyed property. As one informant pointed out, prices for clothes are high, but people would not need to buy them if the military had not burned their homes and destroyed their property.[370]

The high prices and occasional shortages have clearly affected people in the capital and others with financial means. While rural farmers rarely mentioned the sanctions in their interviews, urban residents and well-paid government officials almost inevitably did. For example, the governor of Bururi told Human Rights Watch, "The sanctions have caused problems in the social domain—in the functioning of schools, the medical system runs slowly, construction. There is a lack of supplies. Gasoline is missing to transport food. The major impact is on the population. They can't get seeds to plant. Here people live from agriculture, but they have been affected by the functioning of the social and economic areas. This affects the poor most. It is not the higher-ups who are touched. The governors and ministers can pay for gas."[371] The governor of Kayanza also told Human Rights Watch, "The embargo has touched the little people. Gasoline is very expensive."[372] Food, agricultural products, medicine, and school supplies have not been covered under the embargo since April.

One diplomatic source told Human Rights Watch, "The sanctions may not be sufficient, but they are a thorn in the side of the government. They are a small prod, but they are one of the few we have available to use to pressure the government on issues like regroupment."[373] This claim seems born out by the energy the government has expended in attempting to bring an end to the sanctions. Burundi's prime minister told the world food summit in November 1996 in Rome that the sanctions had had a "devastating effect" on Burundi.[374] In an October 1997 press conference, Prime Minister Pascal Ndimira claimed that the sanctions are the primary source of Burundi's current economic and humanitarian problems,

---

[370]Human Rights Watch interview, Bujumbura, June 1997.

[371]André Ndayizamba, Governor of Bururi, Human Rights Watch interview, Bururi, June 20, 1997.

[372]Human Rights Watch interview with Col. Daniel Negeri in Kayanza, June 24, 1997.

[373]Human Rights Watch interview, Bujumbura, June 1997.

[374]"Burundi Asks End to 'Devastating' Sanctions," Reuters, November 15, 1997.

ignoring the impact of the war and policies such as regroupment.[375] According to a January 1997 U.N. Department of Humanitarian Affairs report, "Burundian officials continue in their two track approach to convince neighboring countries to remove the economic embargo that they have imposed for the last six months. President Buyoya and members of his cabinet have traveled to regional capitals to quietly meet with political leaders to personally press their case for having sanctions removed. Burundian officials have also publicly lashed out at the continued enforcement of sanctions. Burundi's Foreign Minister Luc Rukingama has alleged that some countries imposing sanctions on his country did so in order to prevent peace from ever returning to Burundi."[376]

The sanctions do appear to have pushed the Buyoya regime to moderate some of its policies. A Hutu political official told Human Rights Watch "The embargo has had positive political effects. Immediately after the coup, there was no National Assembly, no political parties.... In reaction to sanctions, those in power were forced to re-establish the assembly and parties. The assembly and parties do not work fully, but they are something. They do not function fully, but there is greater freedom to speak as a result. Even negotiations [with the FDD], which were hard to accept, are a reaction to the sanctions."[377] The regional governments have clearly intended to link the continuation of sanctions to Buyoya's sincere participation in negotiations for a peaceful settlement with the FDD.

It is important to point out that, although the government seeks international support for an end to sanctions by protesting their humanitarian effect, the government has extensively circumvented the sanctions in order to import arms. The minister of the interior, Colonel Epitace Bayaganakandi, complained that the sanctions have had a terrible impact on common people. When Human Rights Watch pointed out that the government was bringing in numerous flights each week to import arms rather than food and other items for the population, Col. Bayaganakandi replied, "First we need to have security before eating five times a

---

[375]Ben Lauwers, "Burundi Embargo causes catastrophe, Prime Minister claims," Reuters, October 2, 1997.

[376]United Nations Department of Humanitarian Affairs, "U.N. Humanitarian Situation Report—Burundi (01/14-28)," January 31, 1997.

[377]Human Rights Watch interview, Bujumbura, June 1997.

day. If people can eat only one meal a day and this can help bring about security, it has to be done."[378]

The United States and the European Union

In contrast to the clear condemnation of Buyoya's coup by Burundi's neighbors, the broader international response to the coup has been more equivocal. Following the coup, the U.S. government failed to issue a strong condemnation. As reported by Donald McNeil in the *New York Times* two weeks after the coup, "U.S. officials seem mildly embarrassed that one of their pupils has ridden a coup to power, but they consistently say the alternatives were worse. Ethnic bloodshed was increasing, Ntibantunganya's government was impotent, and Buyoya's Tutsi military rivals ... are far more bloodthirsty than Buyoya."[379]

Upon taking power, Buyoya did indeed claim to be bringing order back to the country, and discussions with people in the diplomatic community indicate that many believe that he has succeeded. Security conditions for the international community have indeed improved, since the capital Bujumbura, which is now overwhelmingly Tutsi, is calmer and since the regroupment policy drove the FDD out of large parts of the country making travel in those regions easier. For average citizens, however, especially Hutu, life is hardly more secure. Since Buyoya took power, Hutu have faced attack by government troops and serious violations of their civil and political rights. The armed forces may be in greater control of the country, but this has certainly not translated into greater safety for most Hutu, who now live in as much fear of the military and Tutsi militia as they ever have.

In contrast to the general silence with which the international community reacted to the coup, the international response to specific policies of the Buyoya regime has been quite vocal. The United States has taken a leading role in organizing opposition to the policy of regroupment. The U.S. has condemned regroupment and has refused to offer support to what it terms a purely military strategy. In practical terms, this has translated in a refusal to support infrastructural development within the camps which might encourage them to become permanent. In May 1997 USAID administrator Brian Atwood and European Union Commissioner Emma Bonino issued a joint declaration that stated that "The U.S. Agency for International Development (USAID) and the European Community

---

[378]Col. Epitace Bayaganakandi, Minister of the Interior, Human Rights Watch interview, Bujumbura, July 3, 1997.

[379]Donald McNeil, "Burundi in Crisis: America Sits and Watches," *New York Times*, August 4, 1997.

Humanitarian Office (ECHO) deplore the current policy of regroupment being enforced in Burundi and the ensuing disruption of rural life."[380] The statement goes on to say that the two agencies "would not support any efforts to regularize life in the regroupment areas."

The international community has also played a role in supporting negotiations between the parties in the conflict. Following Buyoya's withdrawal from the scheduled talks, Howard Wolpe, President Clinton's special envoy in the Great Lakes, region visited Burundi to add U.S. support to negotiations and to encourage Buyoya to participate.[381] Wolpe returned to the region in early 1998 following an upsurge in violence around Bujumbura.

The United Nations

The United Nations has been very actively involved in Burundi, but the position of the United Nations in relationship to the politics of the country has been ambivalent. While some U.N. officials have condemned certain policies of the Buyoya regime, such as regroupment, others have praised Buyoya for returning calm to Burundi.

The strongest critiques of the Buyoya regime from within the U.N. have come from the U.N. special rapporteur for human rights, Paulo Sergio Pinheiro. He released a report on February 10, 1997, condemning "the intensification of fighting in November and December 1996 that fueled the constant stream of killings and massacres, targeted assassinations, arbitrary arrests, enforced disappearances, looting and acts of banditry and the destruction of private property by both parties to the conflict."[382] The Regional Humanitarian Coordinator for the Great Lakes Region, Martin Griffiths, has also spoken out critically. He characterized

---

[380]USAID and ECHO, "Joint Statement by USAID Administrator Brian Atwood and European Union Commissioner Emma Bonino: Provision of Humanitarian Assistance in Regroupment Camps in Burundi," May 13, 1997.

[381]Ferdinand Bigumandondera, "US Envoy Visits Bujumbura," Panafrican News Agency, August 31, 1997.

[382]United Nations Commission on Human Rights, Second Report on the Human Rights Situation in Burundi submitted by the Special Rapporteur, Mr. Paulo Sergio Pinheiro, in accordance with Commission Resolution 1996/1 (February 10, 1997), para. 10, U.N. Doc. No. E/CN.4/1997/12.

regroupment in March 1997 as a policy of "deep concern to which the international community should be fundamentally opposed."[383]

The U.N. Human Rights Center in Bujumbura, the office of the High Commissioner for Human Rights, has occasionally criticized the regime, but the activities of the agency have been constrained by government resistance and a lack of resources. As the director of the center told Human Rights Watch, however, "Ours is not the same program as a human rights NGO. Our role is not to denounce, but to try to encourage the government to respect its responsibilities."[384] With only twelve observers who face serious limitations on their ability to travel due to security concerns and with considerable resistance from the government, the effectiveness of the program is unclear.

Some U.N. officials have sought to exonerate the Buyoya regime. The country representative for UNICEF attributes continuing insecurity in Burundi not to Buyoya's policies but to his lack of international support. He told Human Rights Watch "Buyoya is beginning to be recognized internationally, but too late."[385] In a publication discussing the conflict in Burundi issued in March 1997, UNICEF called on the international community to get involved in the regroupment camps. It also blamed the sanctions for problems of malnutrition and disease in the camps.[386]

The U.N. has also played a role in encouraging negotiations between the warring parties in the conflict in Burundi. The U.N. special envoy in the Great Lakes, Mohammed Sahnoun, has intervened with both the Buyoya regime and the CNDD to support negotiations for an end to the conflict. After the cancellation of initial peace talks in August 1997, UNESCO sponsored talks in Paris in late September that assembled representatives of the Buyoya regime, the CNDD, and political parties such as Frodebu, Uprona and Parena.[387]

---

[383]United Nations Department Humanitarian Affairs, Integrated Regional Information Network, "Emergency Update on the Great Lakes," no. 121, March 9, 1997.

[384]Human Rights Watch interview, Bujumbura, June 9, 1997.

[385]Human Rights Watch interview, Bujumbura, June 10, 1997.

[386]UNICEF, "The women and Children of Burundi: Hostages to Conflict," (March 1997).

[387] "Burundi parties open peace 'dialogue' in Paris," Agence France Presse, September 26, 1997; Gearge Ola-Davies, "Burundian Rivals Return Home with Little Optimism for Peace," Panafrican News Service, September 29, 1997.